THE POWER OF VISION

GEORGE BARNA

From Gospel Light
Ventura, California, U.S.A.

PUBLISHED BY REGAL BOOKS
FROM GOSPEL LIGHT
VENTURA, CALIFORNIA, U.S.A.
PRINTED IN THE U.S.A.

Regal Books is a ministry of Gospel Light, a Christian publisher dedicated to serving the local church. We believe God's vision for Gospel Light is to provide church leaders with biblical, user-friendly materials that will help them evangelize, disciple and minister to children, youth and families.

It is our prayer that this Regal book will help you discover biblical truth for your own life and help you meet the needs of others. May God richly bless you.

For a free catalog of resources from Regal Books/Gospel Light, please call your Christian supplier or contact us at 1-800-4-GOSPEL *or* www.regalbooks.com.

Library of Congress Cataloging-in-Publication Data
Barna, George.
The power of vision / George Barna.–Updated and rev. ed.
p. cm.
Includes bibliographical references.
ISBN 0-8307-3255-1
1. Christian leadership. I. Title.
BV652.1.B363 2003
253–dc21 2003001006

5 6 7 8 9 10 11 12 13 14 15 16 17 18 / 14 13 12 11 10 09 08 07 06

Rights for publishing this book in other languages are contracted by Gospel Light Worldwide, the international nonprofit ministry of Gospel Light. Gospel Light Worldwide also provides publishing and technical assistance to international publishers dedicated to producing Sunday School and Vacation Bible School curricula and books in the languages of the world. For additional information, visit www.gospellightworldwide.org; write to Gospel Light Worldwide, P.O. Box 3875, Ventura, CA 93006; or send an e-mail to info@gospellightworldwide.org.

Contents

. . . .

ACKNOWLEDGMENTS

In 1983 my wife and I began attending an unusual church near our home which, at that time, was in the western suburbs of Chicago. The church was Willow Creek Community Church, pastored by Bill Hybels. Many elements made that church so unique for Nancy and me. Perhaps the most gripping of those, however, was the unflinching devotion of the church's leaders to their vision for ministry. It was my first introduction to a church that was serving God on the basis of His vision for the congregation.

Willow Creek transformed my life in many ways, not the least of which was calling my attention to the role and importance of vision. Since then I have had the privilege of working with hundreds of churches, parachurch ministries and for-profit corporations, evaluating how vision impacts their work.

This book is the result of those years of study. It has become a passion of mine to see the Church led by true leaders—people who have grasped His vision for their life's ministry and who pour themselves into living the vision.

I wish to thank two groups of people who supported me along the way. Teachers comprise the first group. They are the visionaries who have modeled the process for me or who have exhorted me to investigate it more closely. Although many teachers have been a part of that learning curve, special thanks must go to Bill Hybels, Don Seltzer, Luder Whitlock and Ron Sider for demonstrating vision in ministry. On occasion their actions or words have confounded me. But upon deeper reflection on the circumstances, I always have arrived at an understanding of their motivation by recalling their vision for ministry.

Enablers make up the second group. These are my partners in ministry at the Barna Research Group. The stellar efforts of these colleagues enable me to study the culture, probe organizations, interact with leaders, challenge and consult with ministries and describe some of what I have learned in book form, such as this one. My current core team includes Irene Castillo, Lynn Gravel, Cameron Hubiak, Pam Jacob, David Kinnaman, Dan Parcon, Celeste Rivera and Kim Wilson. I am grateful for their professionalism, dedication and camaraderie.

I am also grateful for my family. My wife, Nancy, has been instrumental in everything that Barna Research and I have produced in the past two decades. She has been personally supportive and professionally indispensable, even as she has scaled back her time within the company to care for our children. My daughters, Samantha and Corban—neither of whom had been born at the time I wrote the original manuscript—are an endless source of love, support and prayer. Together, these three women of God have facilitated my pursuit of the vision that God has given to me for my life. I know that God will honor their investment in our work for the Kingdom.

INTRODUCTION

GOD'S VISION FOR YOUR MINISTRY

It's amazing how significantly things change in a decade—and how much they stay the same.

Prior to the early '90s, relatively few people had written about the importance of vision. Then, without warning, vision became the hottest topic around. Major corporations started searching for leaders who could inspire personnel and investors with a compelling vision of the future. Best-selling business books addressed the topic. Presidential races began to hinge on the articulation of a grand vision for the nation, culminating in Bill Clinton's defeating the incumbent George Bush in November 1992. Political analysts noted that Mr. Bush had derisively—and, in retrospect, unfortunately—dismissed "the vision thing," virtually assuring his defeat by voters who perceived the Republican to be visionless. "Vision" had entered the lexicon of the average person.

But things change slowly in the Church—sometimes for good reason, other times perhaps not so. Thousands of church leaders, aware of the vision revolution occurring in society at large, began to read books on the topic, talked about the matter at conferences and suggested to their congregants that a vision statement was needed. Despite those good intentions, few churches immersed themselves in a true vision-development process that produced a genuine sense of God's vision and a related vision statement. What emerged, for the most part, were committee meetings resulting in refried mission statements or updated strategy statements designed to justify what the church was already doing. God was not at the center of the process, as He must be if we are seeking His vision.

In fact, there was often a serious problem of centricity: In case after case, the outcome of vision-development efforts resulted in the explication of human vision rather than God's vision. This is no minor flaw. As we have seen during this past decade, pouring resources into *our* best ideas can leave a church and its people flat. The decision to ignore God's best ideas is both an act of disobedience (by rejecting His will) and an act of strategic ineptitude (by leaving a myriad of untapped opportunities untapped).

What We Have Learned

Since writing the original manuscript of *The Power of Vision,* I have had the privilege of conducting more than 200,000 interviews with adults, teenagers, pastors, church staff, leaders in business and government and executives of nonprofit and parachurch organizations. That wealth of information has enabled us to draw many conclusions about the church, people's faith and contemporary culture. Not surprisingly, some of those conclusions relate to the continuing significance of vision for the life of the Church. Among those conclusions are:

1. Although they are good people and have been called to ministry, most senior pastors do not have an understanding of God's vision for the ministries they are trying to lead—and, consequently, most churches have little impact in their community or in the lives of their congregants. Not even 1 out of every 10 pastors of Protestant churches can articulate God's vision for their church. Clearly, this is one of the most important areas for growth during the present decade.
2. Most believers know about the concept of vision, but few have God's vision in place in their life and ministry. The observable consequences include people experiencing feelings of

frustration and self-doubt, a slide into spiritual complacency, the degeneration of Christian service ministries, heightened selfishness and the acceptance of mediocrity within the church. As Americans struggle with issues related to purpose, meaning and significance, the heart of the solution will be the discernment of God's vision for their lives; all else limits our potential to be the people God created us to be.

3. Institutions that serve as gatekeepers for the local church, such as seminaries, have moved slowly in response to recent discoveries and insights about vision. For instance, there is still no seminary in the country that uses the explication of one's vision as a filter for acceptance into the school, as a guide to the coursework and program appropriate for a given student, as a criterion for the selection of a student mentor and as an indication of a student's leadership potential. Seminaries play a very useful and important role in the Church; that role could be so much more valuable if God's vision were integrated at the center of the process.
4. Within the local church, few elder boards and search committees rely upon the church's vision as the core filter through which pastoral candidates are screened. Similarly, fewer than 1 out of every 20 Protestant churches use their vision statement as the key to their evaluation process. If God's vision were known and emphasized in such settings, imagine the difference it would make in the focus and influence of these well-intentioned ministries.

In summary, then, although pastors and laity are more aware of the importance of vision for ministry, we are also in more desperate need than ever for a clear understanding of His purpose for each individual church. Posting a two-line mission statement in the weekly program is not good enough, as the evidence clearly shows. After all, every church has basically the same mission (i.e., to help people fulfill the Great Commission and the Great Commandment through effective worship, evangelism, discipleship, stewardship, community service and relationships).

If every church also has the same vision, then God must intend for His churches to compete with each other for resources such as people, money, personnel, property, etc. But that creates an unhealthy in-house desire to "show up" or "defeat" brothers and sisters in Christ, and takes our eyes off both the ultimate prize and the ultimate enemy. In fact, Scripture is quite clear that we are not to compete, but we are to love, assist and serve each other because we are all part of the same body working toward the same goals. Success in the Kingdom is not about our personal or group accomplishments but about how we work together for the greater good and the ends of the Kingdom. Because a God of love and order—not of disharmony and confusion—created us, it is imperative that we grasp His vision for each church that He has called into existence and that we fervently pursue that vision as a necessary addition to the building of God's eternal kingdom according to His perfect purposes.

May God's Vision Reign

There are, of course, thousands and thousands of Christians who are tremendous examples of God's vision focusing and energizing their lives, and whose ministries reflect their commitment to God's purposes. As we have had the chance to interview those individuals, I have seen three common elements. First, they enter the vision-development process uncertain of what they are seeking to do but persuaded they must do something to provide greater clarity for their future. In my experience it seems as if a "holy frustration" has led them to seek something more profound in their efforts at serving God—and He has been waiting and hoping for the opportunity to shape their minds and hearts through vision.

Second, the process extracts a significant cost from vision seekers. They admit that while they were involved in the process, they often questioned whether or not they should continue. But those who endure invariably submit that the result was worth the cost, many times over. As described in this book, devotion to the process of discovering the vision is perhaps the most important component in all of the activities associated with God's vision, for He takes greater joy in our getting to know Him and deciding that He is worthy of such devotion than in all of our efforts to facilitate great outcomes for His purposes. As an omnipotent being, He really doesn't *need* our efforts as much as He *desires* to know us and desires for us to know Him deeply, sincerely and joyfully. The vision journey is a major step in that process.

Third, those who persevere and arrive at an understanding of God's vision, and then devote themselves to implementing it, experience outcomes they never could have foreseen without God's vision as the heartbeat of their ministry. God's vision is beyond our comprehension and certainly beyond our grasp; it is only through His empowerment that we see and accomplish the vision.

Many people have stopped me during the past decade to thank me for writing this book. Often they recount stories of how the vision has changed their lives and those of many other people. What a joy it is to hear such tales! But here's my confession: I don't feel that I wrote this book.

Now don't go jumping to conclusions before I finish: I don't believe in the all-too-common practice of ghostwriting; I pounded out every word that wound up in the final manuscript. But writing this book was such a different and memorable experience for me because never before—or since—have I had a book that seemed to be written *through* me rather than *by* me. During that week of writing, it often seemed as if I were having something akin to an out-of-body experience, watching my fingers type in word after word and reading the text with admiration. Without wanting to overstate the case, let me simply say that this book is one of my proudest offerings to the Lord—largely because I know how deeply integrated He was in the writing process. When people give me compliments for the book, it is simply confirmation that the Lord wanted to get these thoughts into the minds and hearts of some of His people, and I was the available scribe of the moment. What a privilege that was and continues to be.

I pray that you will be challenged by the simple truths and principles contained within these pages. There are no deep philosophical statements or complex strategic theories. It is a simple idea: God created you,

He has called you to a specific ministry, and He wants to impart to you His idea of what that ministry is and how best to accomplish His perfect outcomes through you. That's what His vision is about: maximizing your God-given potential to bless God and others through your commitment to doing His work, His way. We all need His vision. Imagine what the world and the Church would be like if we all took our direction from Him for the sole purpose of serving Him! What a different—and wonderful—world it would be.

George Barna
Oceanside, California
January 2003

1

MASTERS OF VISION

CHAPTER HIGHLIGHTS

- Vision transcends time. True visionaries have much in common regardless of when they live.
- As people of God seek to lead their churches, grasping God's vision for their ministry requires an investment in the vision.
- Those whom God chooses to use as leaders can be effective regardless of their lack of worldly qualifications.

Chapter 1
Masters of Vision

Is vision a new concept? Take a look at one first-century visionary.

> Five times my own people gave me thirty-nine lashes with a whip. Three times the Romans beat me with a big stick, and once my enemies stoned me. I have been shipwrecked three times, and I even had to spend a night and a day in the sea. During my many travels, I have been in danger from rivers, robbers, my own people, and foreigners. My life has been in danger in cities, in deserts, at sea, and with people who only pretended to be the Lord's followers. I have worked and struggled and spent many sleepless nights. I have gone hungry and thirsty and often had nothing to eat. I have been cold from not having enough clothes to keep me warm (2 Cor. 11:24-27, *CEV*).

This is the story of the apostle Paul. This is not the tale of a man who had nothing better to do with his life or who had no other options. Paul was well educated, articulate, a leader. By virtue of his background, he was a man with options. Yet he was determined to serve Jesus Christ, a spiritual leader he had sought to persecute, and to endure outrageous suffering and personal sacrifice as a result of this turnabout. It was a conscious, startling, incredible decision. For what reason?

Paul was an individual driven to fulfill a vision for ministry that God had entrusted to him.

Paul gives us glimpses of his comprehension of the vision for ministry that God had prepared for him. In 2 Timothy 1:11 he indicates the nature of his calling: His work is to be "a preacher, an apostle, and a teacher" *(NKJV)*. In other letters Paul outlines aspects of his vision for ministry. It is in the Acts of the Apostles, though, where we gain the clearest insight into God's vision for Paul's ministry.

Throughout the latter half of the book of Acts, we see Paul preaching, teaching, admonishing and planting churches with the kind of fervor not found in a person who is simply earning a wage. Paul, convinced of God's design for his life, worked tirelessly to do God's calling. Paul was compelled by God's vision to commit his life to working out that vision in his daily life.

A Precedent for Passion

Paul's passion was not without precedent, however. Hundreds of years earlier, another young man had a similar vision of how his life could count for the glory of his God. David became the second king of Israel, described as a man after God's own heart. Or, put another way, David was a man who had grasped God's vision for his life, a man whose service and worship exemplified the spirit and commitment of a person in deep relationship with God and who was devoted to carrying out the special tasks God had ordained for him.

In time, David replaced Saul as king, albeit reluctantly. It became necessary to remove Saul from his exalted post of leadership because he lacked God's vision for ministry. Instead, he viewed his position in human terms and attempted to serve in his own strength. His conduct so disgusted God that the prophet Samuel, who had anointed Saul to be king, eventually had to break the news to Saul that his self-reliance and consequent lack of obedience had caused him to fall out of God's favor and to be replaced as king (see 1 Sam. 13:14).

David, in contrast, reflected the humility, obedience, compassion and dedication to God that marks a true visionary leader in the church. You cannot read the psalms attributed to David without being struck by his passion to know and serve God. You cannot overlook the clear sense of the future that God had instilled within him. Like all visionary leaders, David was human and, as such, made mistakes. But one of his redeeming qualities was his burning desire to remain true to the vision for the future that God had placed in his heart, which God allowed him to work toward despite the frailties of his human nature.

Other biblical figures emerge as people moved by God's vision for their lives and ministries. Nehemiah was responsible for the rebuilding of the walls of Jerusalem, risking death at the hands of King Artaxerxes and various enemy tribes. His bold speech, his courageous confrontations with his opponents and his insightful instructions to the Jews who struggled with him to rebuild the holy city were a testimony to the vision for ministry he had received from God. After an intense period of mourning,

The vision entrusted to Moses did not focus on selfish desires but on a selfless quest to reconcile the world to its Creator.

weeping, fasting and prayer, Nehemiah received from God a clear vision of how he was to direct his life in the service of God. Far from succumbing to the fear of abdicating his comfortable life in the king's court and reconstructing the centerpiece of the Jewish community in the heartland of their enemies, Nehemiah stood firm on the basis of the vision—the very work that "my God had put in my heart to do for Jerusalem" (Neh. 2:12).

Moses, a most unlikely candidate for greatness, received a clear call from God to serve Him in a special way. Like all true visions imparted by God, the vision entrusted to Moses did not focus upon satisfying people's selfish desires but upon a selfless quest to reconcile the world to its Creator. Even though Moses had been abandoned by his parents, was guilty of murder and was living in exile, God designated Moses to lead Israel to the Promised Land in order to spare His people from oppression at the hands of Egyptians. In that process, Moses lived a nomadic, uncomfortable life for four decades, leading an unruly, disrespectful, unhappy, whining band of people through times of sacrifice, doubt, pain and discomfort. But driven by God's vision for leading those people, Moses remained a faithful servant of God.

MODERN VISIONARIES

Vision has flourished even beyond the lives of biblical characters. In our own century, there are numerous examples of people who, by human standards, showed little promise for greatness and little hope of being able to change the lives of people around the world. But these people, having captured God's vision for ministry, have lived with power and energy that undeniably transcend their natural capacities and with an intensity of commitment that far exceeds anything they had previously demonstrated in their lives. The results of their efforts further expose the power of God at work within them.

An Undeniable Transformation

The diminutive Albanian woman we remember today as Mother Teresa was nothing more than average early in her life. Her colleagues in the convent have remarked that she was nothing special as a student, as a leader or as a woman seeking to please God. However, after years of prayer and a spirit broken by Him, she emerged as a figure to be reckoned with; she moved beyond complacency to a deep compassion for the poorest of the poor. Summoning courage unfamiliar to her, she requested that her religious order permit her to initiate a ministry in India to care for those who were so sick that no other people or organizations bothered to care for them.

Why risk her life and the few human comforts she knew to begin a life of even greater sacrifice and ignominy? Because she felt a special calling from God to reach out to love the unlovable. She could very easily have continued her ministry as a nun, teaching in schools, leading young women to consider a relationship with Christ, even directing some special students toward a vocational ministry. Nobody would have questioned her love for God, her commitment to His kingdom or her selflessness as a nun.

Yet, she knew that God had reached out to her with a special vision for what she could do to impact people's lives for His glory. And what an impact she had, one that exceeded her innate intellect, courage and physical strength. She felt compelled to change the lives of people because God gave her a special vision for outreach.

A Dream, a Vision

Martin Luther King, Jr., was a Baptist preacher in the South. While he was regarded as a powerful orator, nothing in his background—academic prowess, family connections, political skills, church growth statistics—indicated that he was an emerging leader, a crusader to be reckoned with. However, God worked through King to convert him into a servant with a larger calling: to erase the injuries and injustice of race-based hatred and prejudice.

God reached out to Mother Teresa with a special vision for what she could do to impact people's lives for His glory.

Much like the apostle Paul, King endured beatings, time in jail, slander, hunger, financial loss and other inequities solely because of his quest to serve God. Driven by God's vision for his ministry, King encountered unbelievable hardships but stayed true to his calling until he was killed by an assassin's bullet. Sociologists and historians concur that of the many changes that redefined America during the turbulent 1960s, one of the most significant and far reaching was the civil rights movement that King headed.

Vision for Growth

Donald McGavran was a missionary to India. In the early 1950s he returned to the United States for further study of missions with a keen interest in discovering what types of outreach did and did not work effectively. He began to see ways in which the insights he had gained in the mission field could be applied to the American church. He detailed his ideas in a series of writings that eventually became the basis for what is now known as the church growth movement. Many church leaders today accept these principles as a matter of course.

During the 1950s, however, McGavran was ridiculed for his ideas and occasionally was asked to leave the fraternity of career ministers. Undaunted, he continued to teach and to write about his ideas, convinced that God had placed him in these circumstances to enhance the spiritual life of the American church. What was the strength that supported him during these years of travail? Vision for ministry was his motivation and his source of strength in the face of controversy and rejection by colleagues.

Vision for Reaching Harry and Mary

One of the best-known church leaders in America today is Bill Hybels. Thousands of pastors and lay leaders travel to Willow Creek Community Church every year to witness the miracle that meets every weekend in South Barrington, Illinois. With a church body that exceeds 16,000 people, Willow Creek is a unique and inspiring example of a church that can be relevant without compromising the gospel.

In its early days, though, what is commonly referred to today as the Willow Creek model represented a radically different vision for the development of a church-based ministry. In spite of the acclaim the church receives today, don't assume that fellow ministers and observers of the church scene stood by passively and applauded what Hybels and his team of young leaders were seeking to do. Through efforts to reach Unchurched Harry and Unchurched Mary, the fictional characters described as the target audience, Hybels has been God's chosen instrument to instill a passion in the hearts of thousands of believers to reach out to the unchurched and unsaved people in the area. Without grasping God's vision for the unique ministry reflected in Willow Creek's services and structure, however, that model for contemporary ministry might never have seen the light of day. And thousands of people may never have come to know Christ as a result of that ministry.

We could, of course, examine countless examples of leaders driven by God's vision for ministry. In each case, we would discover that God supplies the vision.

The Underlying Basics

In every case I have studied, the vision entrusted to the leader was not a simple matter of God paving the way to do what came naturally or easily to the leader. Invariably, as true people of God seek to lead their churches, grasping God's vision for their ministry requires them to invest in the vision by attaining the vision itself as well as by implementing the vision.

Finally, it seems apparent to me that not every person is called to be a leader. However, those whom God chooses to use as leaders can be effective, regardless of their lack of worldly qualifications. If you are like most full-time ministers of the gospel, you occasionally have doubts as to whether God made a mistake allowing you to be in a position of leadership. Those doubts are valuable, for they keep you asking the types of questions that sharpen your skills and soften your heart. It is that kind of self-examination that prevents us from becoming megalomaniacs, convinced of our own self-sufficiency and always ready to take credit for progress made in relation to ministry. As long as the doubt does not become paralyzing, it performs a useful function in the development process.

But the best response to any self-doubt is to determine the source of the vision for your ministry. Was it a vision you developed with the gifts and talents God gave you, or was it a vision that you sought, prayed and waited for and then received from Him? Chances are that if you do not yet have His vision for your ministry, either you have not made the investment required to capture that vision, or you are not gifted as a leader. Both cases mandate immediate and decisive action on your part. Without vision, the last place you ought to be is in a leadership post, regardless of the underlying reason. Only you can deal with that condition.

2

What Is Vision?

Chapter Highlights

- Vision is clear.
- Vision is preferable to the current state.
- Vision concentrates on the future.
- Vision is from God.
- Vision is a gift to leaders that is tailored to their circumstances.
- Vision reflects a realistic perspective.
- Vision is dreaming the most *possible* dream.
- Vision is built on reality.
- A visionary pastor is a successful pastor.

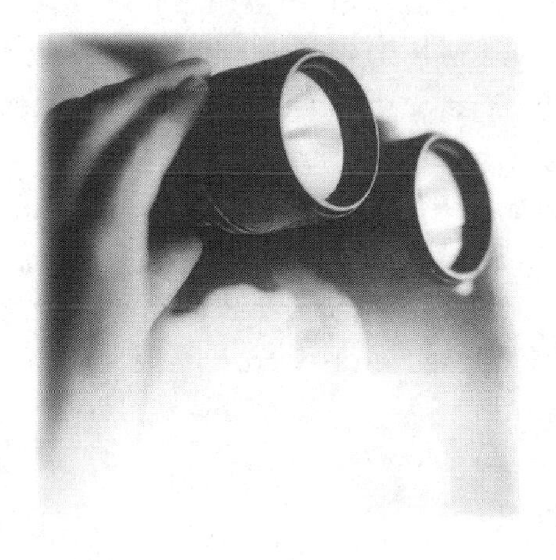

Chapter 2

What Is Vision?

Duke Ellington, the late jazz musician, composer and renowned bandleader, was once asked to provide a definition of rhythm. "If you got it," he replied, "you don't need no definition. And if you don't have it, ain't no definition gonna help."

Vision, thankfully, is not quite as elusive. However, I believe Ellington's definition can be adapted slightly to help us understand one reality regarding vision: Once you have it, you know it; but when you don't have it, you aren't sure what it will be like.

Vision Defined

You might define vision as foresight with insight based on hindsight. This definition underscores the importance of looking to the future, emphasizes the significance of possessing a keen awareness of current circumstances and possibilities and notes the value of learning from the past. Nevertheless, this definition is somewhat imprecise.

One church leader told me that he believed vision was "seeing the invisible and making it visible." Another leader suggested that his working definition was "vision is an informed bridge from the present to the future." Still another pastor used the expression "sanctified dreams" to convey what the term meant to him.

Let me suggest a more staid, but hopefully a more precise, definition. Vision for ministry is a clear mental image of a preferable future imparted by God to His chosen servants and is based upon an accurate understanding of God, self and circumstances. Consider the components of this definition.

A Clear Mental Image

Vision is a picture held in your mind's eye of the way things could or should be in the days ahead. Vision connotes a visual reality, a portrait of conditions that do not exist currently. This picture is internalized and personal. It is not somebody else's view of the future but one that uniquely belongs to you. Eventually, you will have to paint that mental portrait for others if you wish the vision to materialize in your church. Just as you have used your imagination to create this view of the future, you will have to lead others to catch the same vision so that they, too, might share in its implementation and impact. Thus, having a clear picture in mind is essential. A fuzzy perspective is not vision.

A Preferable Change

In suggesting that vision deals with that which is preferable, we are insinuating that vision entails change. Vision is never about maintaining the status quo. Vision is about stretching reality to extend beyond the existing state. Thus, vision is required even when the church is in a good position; vision is not just for churches that are struggling with their present state. To create a better situation in which to minister, you can either rely upon random circumstance and hope that the result is better than what has existed, or you can assert control over your environment, based on God's empowerment and direction, and make a better future. Vision is about pursuing the latter approach.

A Future Focus

Vision concentrates on the future. It focuses on thinking ahead rather than on dwelling upon or seeking to replicate the past. How many churches do you know that bemoan their current state of affairs, yearning for a return to the glory days of the past? None of those churches will extricate themselves from the lethargy or the downward spiral they are experiencing. The means to success in ministry is to focus upon God and to be committed fully to His vision for your ministry and to what He will do with you and through you in the future.

An Impartation by God

Vision for ministry is a reflection of what God wants to accomplish through you to build His kingdom. Rather than rely upon the abilities of humans to concoct a view of, and to plan for, the future, God conveys

His view of that future to a leader. The future of the Church and of the people whom God has placed on this earth are simply too important to Him to allow people to lean on their own innate abilities and talents to

Vision for ministry is a reflection of what God wants to accomplish through you to build His kingdom.

develop half-baked schemes for reaching the world. While He allows us ample latitude and creativity to articulate, disseminate and implement the vision, make no mistake about it: Visionary leaders receive their vision for ministry from God.

A Chosen Leader

Leadership is critical within the church. God has gifted certain individuals to serve as leaders. It is to those people that He can entrust one of His most precious and treasured gifts: vision. Only a leader knows what to do with vision. Only a leader can marshal the resources necessary to bring life to the vision. God chooses those leaders carefully and provides each of them with a vision tailored to his or her circumstances.

Requirements for Vision

Vision reflects a realistic perspective. Vision is not dreaming the impossible dream, but dreaming the most possible dream. Vision stretches our abilities, including our ability to dream, but it is not pie-in-the-sky daydreaming. Vision entails a great depth of understanding, a detailed knowledge of facts and potential. It is not a wild-eyed scheme born in a vacuum; rather, it is a notion of what could occur and is deeply rooted in reality.

Comprehending God

In the definition of vision, God is listed first among the sources of insight and among those realities that we must seek to fully comprehend. We are striving to capture an understanding of His will for our ministry based upon His perspective. He is first and foremost in the vision process.

Knowing Thyself

In developing vision, you must know your own abilities, gifts, limitations, values and desires before you can accurately arrive at a perspective on His vision for your ministry. Vision is not an exercise in promoting yourself, your dreams or your needs. It involves integrating your personal abilities and limitations within God's plan to accomplish what needs to be done through His chosen people.

Understanding Your Circumstances

Dreams shun reality; vision builds upon it. God's vision for your ministry is sensitive to the operational environment He has called you to influence. While He will not limit your potential by suggesting that future reality cannot grow beyond past or present reality, He is the God of consistency and order, not a God of chaos and confusion. You must, therefore, have a firm grasp on existing and potential needs, conditions, competition, opportunities, barriers and potential if you wish to absorb His vision for your ministry.

In using this definition, you recognize that it is a process of applied, pragmatic imagination. It is an articulated intention to do something significant and unique, creating a new reality that improves upon that which exists today, a new world ordained by God for His people to bring to life.

Pastors, Visionary Leaders

Pastors who actively seek to fulfill God's vision for their ministry are a treasure for the church. They are leaders driven not by a need for self-aggrandizement or ego gratification but by a burning desire to see God's will done to its fullest. They are pastors who have blended their vision for personal ministry with the vision imparted by God for the churches they lead. Their churches will accomplish something unique, meaningful and special because the Holy Spirit has enabled them to capture an image of the future and to chart a course of action to reach that goal.

The Big Picture

Because they know where they and the church are headed, they are able to convert the vision into a tangible strategy for implementation. Keeping their minds set on the envisioned end result, they create language, emotions, strategies, plans, policies and structures that facilitate the desired outcome. They gain energy neither from the plaudits of people nor from the tangible evidence of worldly progress but from the knowledge that they are effectively carrying out the vision that God has entrusted to them.

While other pastors bemoan the complacency and stagnation in their congregations, visionary pastors weep gently for their counterparts, knowing that those bodies are doomed to continued inefficiency and immobility because they lack leaders who are fully committed to God. It is not with a haughty spirit that they acknowledge this reality but with a heart broken by the recognition that many committed people of God will experience constant frustration because their church lacks a sense of direction, excitement about the future and a distinctiveness about ministry that energizes the congregation. These qualities are hallmarks of churches led by pastors who relentlessly pursue God's vision for the church.

The Visionary Mentor

Often, visionary pastors reach out to help other pastors by working with them individually or by conducting church-related conferences. Their motivation is generally not to have yet another teaching ministry or to seize a larger share of the spotlight. They are stimulated to another level of leadership—ministry to the ministers—by the gnawing pain in their hearts, knowing why many churches are lifeless and stagnant.

The Surrendered Heart

Visionary pastors are leaders who have surrendered the sense of personal ambition that drives so many pastors. Instead, the natural tendency for self-promotion has been replaced by an urgent need to seek God's glory by doing His work, His way, according to His vision.

Gone is the drudgery of following old models that have become mired in mindless tradition and meaningless routine. Gone is the pressure of having to search constantly for new means to progress, new gimmicks to motivate people to action. Gone are the anxieties about having to please elder boards, denominational executives, major donors and the

Visionary pastors often reach out to other pastors by working with them individually or through church-related conferences.

mass media. The future belongs to visionary pastors because they will define the future. It is the power of God working through churches led by visionaries that causes that image of the future to become reality.

The Vision Statement, A Vital Tool

Visionary leaders also know the importance of a vision statement: a succinct articulation of God's vision for their ministry. As you read the real-life vision statements that follow this section, remember they represent God's vision for other bodies of believers. They are different from what He is calling you to accomplish.

Occasionally pastors from other churches who read those statements are honest enough to say, "Those sure don't sound motivating or compelling to me." Chances are that when other persons read the statement that you and the Lord have worked so long and hard to perfect and that you believe is qualified for this year's Pulitzer Prize, they will react in the same manner to your vision statement.

Think about movie reviews. Perhaps you watched a particular movie and thought it was a moving, meaningful, magnificently produced film. Upon returning home, you might turn on the television and witness a scathing review of that movie by a respected film reviewer. How could such a discrepancy exist?

The reviewer did not have your experiences, your context for understanding, your emotional filter or your expectations for the film. In a sense, he or she was simply not qualified to offer a review that should shape your thoughts and behavior relative to the movie.

Similarly, when you examine the vision statement of another church, it would take more than a cursory reading of that paragraph to understand what went into the statement, why the vision has meaning and whether it has the power to motivate a congregation.

Do not be too tough on the vision statements of other churches. Also, be wise enough to recognize the difference between a vision statement and mission statement. Be sensitive enough to learn new ideas for communicating a vision from those who have trod the path before you. And be wary of imitating too closely the words and concepts incorporated into the vision statements of other leaders or churches.

Samples of Vision Statements

Here are a few vision statements from churches where the vision is in place, is being implemented and is inspiring the church to reach greater heights. Because there is no such thing as the right way to write a vision statement—the process is more art than science—each has its own unique characteristics in substance and in style. (In chapter 10 we will examine specific steps for capturing and creating a vision statement.)

- To develop a ministry that addresses the needs of Xers in the northern suburbs, relating to them regarding faith matters primarily at work and at play, with regular gatherings of the community of faith for worship, discipleship and service
- To equip professionals in the city to impact their web of relationships, reaching non-Christians through cell groups and marketplace ministries that address urban needs
- To engage non-Christians who have no church background in church-planting efforts, designing the ministry around their interests, lifestyles and skills, using small midweek meetings

that combine believers and nonbelievers to pursue intimacy with God and the Bible

- To build a truly multicultural, multigenerational congregation focused on demonstrating love regardless of personal background, and taking community leadership on issues of social justice and fairness
- To provide a safe haven for highly educated professionals in the western tier, offering events and relationships that create spiritual unity and depth, enabling them to use their cultural influence for Christ
- To foster an environment of servanthood in which our congregation brings together all churches in the community to understand each other, work in harmony and share resources toward the expansion of the Kingdom
- To build up families by gearing all ministry to create parental capacity, healthy parent-child relationships, spiritually minded young people and families with spiritual depth and focus
- To have a tightly connected, multigenerational congregation in which people of a given generation mentor someone of the subsequent generation, allowing individuals of all generations to consistently and significantly relate to both younger and older individuals on all matters of faith and lifestyle.

3

Don't Confuse Vision with Mission

Chapter Highlights

- Vision and mission are related but distinct.
- Mission is a general statement of ministry objectives; it is philosophic.
- Vision is a specific, detailed statement of direction and uniqueness; it is strategic.

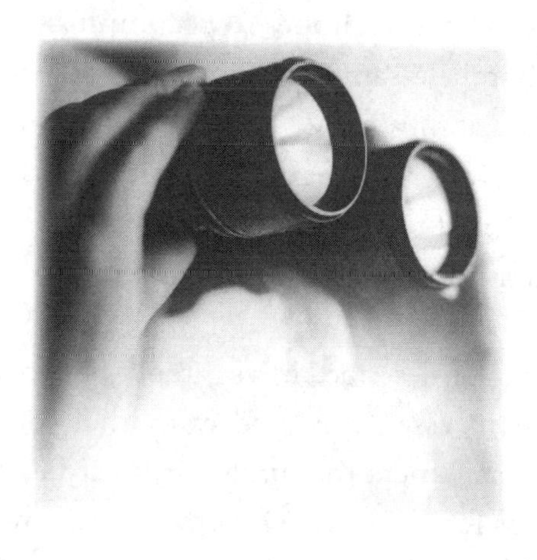

CHAPTER 3

DON'T CONFUSE VISION WITH MISSION

During the last several years, I have worked closely with dozens of churches across the nation. One of the indicators I use to gain some insight into the condition of the church is to measure the state of the vision. In those churches where a sense of God's vision for ministry truly exists, the probability of growth and impact are high. In churches where the vision is absent, growth is thwarted by many roadblocks.

Sadly, the majority of churches I have studied have confused mission and vision. For some reason, most pastors equate the two. They believe that the two terms are interchangeable.

They are not.

The mission statement is a definition of the key ministry objectives of the church. The vision statement is a clarification of the specific direction and activities the church will pursue toward making a true ministry impact.

MISSION OUTLINES OBJECTIVES

A mission statement is a broad, general statement about who you wish to reach and what the church hopes to accomplish. It is very likely that many churches share the same mission and could even use the same wording of that mission. Why? Because the mission is basically a definition of ministry. It is not geared to uniqueness or distinctives or direction. It is designed to reflect hearts turned to God in service and obedience in which the church is a vehicle used to unite people to do His will.

Your mission can be described in a sentence or two. Often, you can use a slogan to capture its essence. But be aware that your mission is essentially a philosophic statement that undergirds the heart of your ministry.

What often pass for vision statements are really mission statements. Examples that might ring a bell include the following:

- To know Him and make Him known
- To enable people to worship, evangelize, disciple and experience community
- To evangelize, exalt, edify and equip

Sometimes churches use a statement they call vision, but which is neither vision nor mission. These statements are too narrow and incomplete to be mission, and not sufficiently unique and specific to be vision.

A mission statement is a general statement about who you wish to reach and what the church hopes to accomplish.

For instance, some widely used phrases that are neither mission nor vision include the following:

- To create fully devoted followers of Christ
- To take Christ to the world
- To reach the lost at any cost
- To save the unsaved

Vision Is Specific

Vision is specific, detailed, customized, distinctive and unique to a given church. It allows a leader to say no to opportunities, provides direction, empowers people for service and facilitates productivity.

The mission statements listed above do not meet these criteria. They are helpful and laudable statements. They play a valuable role in defining the basic stance of the church and its intentions. But mission statements are too vague to provide much direction or to motivate people to become enthusiastic about the ministry.

Knowing the content of the mission statement generally enables a person to feel confident that the church is Christian and is ministry minded. The vision statement puts feet on the mission, detailing how the church will influence the world in which it will minister.

A vision statement details how the church expects to influence the world in which it will minister.

Thus, while the mission statement is philosophic in nature, the vision statement is strategic in character.

Test Your Statement

You may have a statement that you call your vision statement. Perhaps you are beginning to wonder if it is really a mission statement or a vision statement. How can you tell?

One method would be to reflect upon what it took for you to arrive at the statement. If it was basically a copy of the usual aims of a church, it is definitely not a vision statement. If you developed it after spending some time personally reflecting upon your circumstances and what you wanted to see the church accomplish, that also sounds like something other than a vision statement. If you can make decisions in ministry without ever worrying about the substance of the statement, then that, too, sounds like a description of something other than God's vision for your ministry.

Another means of determining the status of the statement would be to put it to the test. Subject it to the questions listed below. If all or most of the answers are no, what you have is probably a definition of your mission rather than a statement of God's vision for your ministry.

- If someone contacted your church regarding involvement in what seemed like a reasonable ministry opportunity, is the statement specific enough to permit you to have a ministry-oriented reason to reject that opportunity and to explain the reasoning for the rejection?

- Does the statement include information which, when compared to the vision statements of other nearby churches, clearly sets your church apart in a significant manner?
- Does the statement identify a target audience whom you hope to impact through the church's ministry?
- Is the statement one that points the ministry in a clear and unique direction for the future?
- Does the statement lead to a precise understanding regarding the strategies and tactics that are permissible in ministry?
- Does the statement provide focus for the ministry so that people are excited about being involved in the work of the church?
- Does the statement prevent the church from seeking to be all things to all people?
- Have any inactive Christians who regularly attend the church become excited about the prospects for ministry after being exposed to the statement?

These are some of the questions that might help you distinguish a mission statement from a vision statement. Take the time to make sure that you are not confusing the two. And if you conclude that what you have is a mission statement—or some other description that is not a vision statement—begin the vision-grasping process as soon as possible to prevent your ministry from meandering aimlessly in the days ahead.

4

Myths That Mar Vision

Chapter Highlights

- Vision and mission are not the same.
- All leaders are visionaries, but all pastors are not leaders.
- Vision creates the future.
- A visionary leader is a change agent.
- The goal of vision is to glorify God.
- For vision to have impact, it must be shared.
- Every church's vision is unique.
- Vision challenges a congregation.

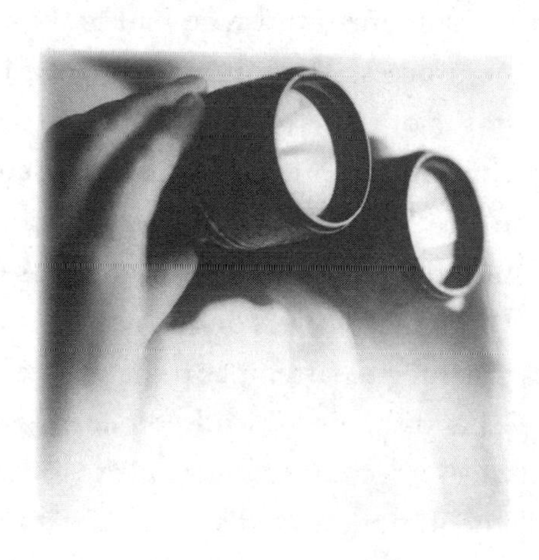

CHAPTER 1

MYTHS THAT MAR VISION

The confusion that arises when mission is mistaken for vision is the myth that most frequently comes to mind when discussing this topic. In many cases, the two terms are interchangeable in the minds of church leaders. Other myths arise over authorship of a vision statement. To follow such myths in the visionary search can cause great injury to a church.

Several years ago, for example, a church embarked upon the process of determining its vision for ministry. The church waited and waited for the minister to produce the vision statement. Unfortunately, two things occurred. First, the minister abdicated his leadership role to lay leaders in the church, which meant that he was not really leading the church. Second, because the process was handled by a committee, the statement was consensual and vague.

After nearly two years, a mission rather than a vision statement was drafted, and even though a diligent effort was made to share it with the congregation, the mission statement failed to motivate the people.

The results were disappointing to church leaders who thought they had developed a vision statement but who had broken three of the principles involved in the process. The church continued to lose membership, the financial status of the church continued to weaken and what once was a strong community outreach ministry deteriorated because people who were on fire for ministry were uncertain about the direction in which the church was heading. Many of those leaders migrated to other churches, and the entire congregation experienced turmoil stemming from its misdirected attempts to develop a vision statement.

We could easily spend the next hundred pages dismissing the myriad of myths that have emerged in relation to the meaning, the development and the implementation of God's vision for ministry. Let's briefly examine 20 of the more widely accepted of these myths.

MYTH 1

Vision should be the result of a consensus among the church's key leaders regarding future activity by the church.

REALITY

Vision is not the result of consensus; it should result *in* consensus.

In a church, it is important that people own the vision for ministry, not that they create it. The creative function of church members relates to ministry plans—that is, strategies and tactics—that are a consequence of the vision. Grasping God's vision for the church's ministry is not a committee process.

Vision and mission are synonymous.

REALITY

While vision relates to specific actions, mission relates to general approaches to action.

When we speak about vision for ministry, we are alluding to a future-based, detailed, unique perspective on the church's calling. When we address mission for ministry, we are speaking of a broad-based definition of the reason for existence that undergirds everything the church does and stands for. While vision relates to specific actions, mission relates to general approaches to action.

Every church should have a mission statement and a vision statement. The two are inextricably related but are clearly distinct. Mission precedes vision, but without vision, it is empty and incomplete.

Some leaders are visionaries, some aren't.

REALITY

By definition, all leaders are visionaries.

We have to make a distinction between someone who holds the position of leader and an individual who behaves as a leader. Many churches are led by individuals who hold a leadership post or title. What truly identifies people as leaders, though, is not their title but their mind-set and actions. Similarly, a common characteristic of all true leaders is that they have vision. A godly leader is one who operates from a base of God's vision for his or her ministry.

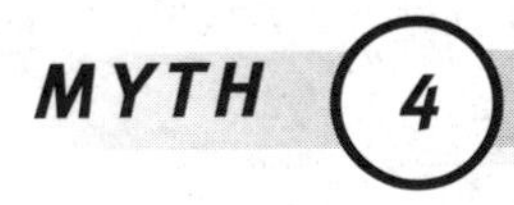

The purpose of vision is to estimate future realities and then to operate effectively within those parameters.

REALITY

The purpose of vision is to create the future.

The objective is not to acquiesce to a preordained future but to create the future. The vision is the means to define the parameters within which the future will emerge. Realize that the future is not something that just happens; it is a reality that is created by those strong enough to exert control over their environment. The future is not a done deal waiting for response. The future belongs to God and through Him to those who are driven to shape it.

Strategy and vision are often confused. In reality, vision is conceptual; strategy is practical and detailed.

REALITY

Vision is conceptual, but it also is practical and detailed.

This perspective on vision is a classic myth: It is part truth and part fabrication. In fact, the words "vision" and "strategy" are frequently used interchangeably, but they are not interchangeable. Vision is conceptual, but it also is practical and detailed. The detail inherent within strategy is a reflection of a strong vision, one that encompasses a detailed view of what will be in the days ahead. Strategy may be detailed in nature, but it also must be general enough to permit the development of specific tactics that will lead to the implementation of the vision through strategic and tactical imperatives.

MYTH 6

Real vision protects the church from risk.

REALITY

Risk is a natural and unavoidable outgrowth of vision.

The myth that real vision protects the church from risk is a comforting thought but is absolutely antithetical to the true nature of vision. Even God's vision for ministry places the church at risk. Because vision relates to change in the creation of the future, risk is a natural and unavoidable outgrowth of vision. However, when a church operates on the basis of God's vision for ministry, it can be assured that He will not put it in a position of unwarranted risk. The visionary leader is one who is a change agent. In the process of pushing the church forward, the leader insists on aggressive effort; remaining stationary is tantamount to losing ground. Without risk, no progress can be made.

The goal of vision for church ministry is numerical growth.

REALITY

The absolute goal of vision for ministry is to glorify God.

While many people believe that numerical growth is the ultimate goal of vision, such expansion is an artifact of the process, not its focal point.

The absolute goal of vision for ministry is to glorify God. It is more important to have a church of committed followers of Christ than to have a church swelled with numbers of social Christians, nominal Christians or Christians who demonstrate no evidence of growth in their relationship with God. If the vision is truly from God, it is one that will push the church forward toward ends that satisfy Him rather than meet standards that result in hosannas from the world.

As long as the senior pastor has a sense of vision, it doesn't matter whether the people really know or understand it. They will be swept along by the force of the vision, regardless.

REALITY

Vision has no force, power or impact unless it spreads from the visionary to the visionless.

A mark of a great leader is the ability not only to capture the vision, but also to articulate it and to cause people to embrace it fully. Because vision concerns action, it is imperative that the vision be cast in such a way that people understand and can respond to it. Vision is not to be jealously guarded, a perspective to be protected. For the vision to have impact, it must be a shared vision.

MYTH 9

The best way to capture vision for ministry is to copy the vision articulated by another respected leader.

REALITY

The leader who takes a "me too" approach in defining vision is neither operating on the power of God's leading nor demonstrating a capacity for authentic leadership.

In the same way that one manufacturer cannot mimic the plans and strategies of its competitors and hope to remain viable, a leader cannot find a niche and make a lasting impact by simply copying the vision of other leaders. Every leader has different gifts, talents and resources, and a unique calling. What works for one leader in his or her particular circumstances is not likely to work for another leader who is immersed in an entirely different set of circumstances. Naturally, two leaders in vastly differing circumstances may have the same mission in ministry; however, God is not likely to commit them to the same vision. God is creative and powerful enough to develop a unique and significant vision for every ministry in place today.

MYTH 10

Because of the breadth and challenge that is reflected by God's vision for ministry, vision is likely to make the laity fearful, skeptical and anxious.

REALITY

Vision, when properly articulated, does not make people afraid or doubtful.

Ineffective communication of true vision is often the reason why it fails to attract people to the ministry or renders them powerless for fear of failure. Vision, when properly articulated, has just the opposite effect on people: It increases their confidence, satisfactorily addresses existing concerns and instills a feeling of excitement and anticipation. Contrary to many people's assumptions, a congregation of believers is more likely to become galvanized by a significant and purposeful challenge than to be threatened or divided by it.

MYTH 11

It is reasonable to expect most of the Christian churches in a community to have the same vision for ministry.

REALITY

It would be absolutely unreasonable for churches to have the same visions for ministry within the same marketplace.

What often happens is that a number of churches serving the same geographic area will share a common mission. Most of the churches, not comprehending the distinction between vision and mission, expect their mission statement to do double duty, serving as the vision and mission. Unfortunately, this approach does not work. Those churches are simply attempting to carry out a mission without God's vision.

It would be unreasonable for churches to have the same visions for ministry within the same marketplace. Why? Because God is not redundant, nor does He need to assign the same task to a number of different congregations in the hope that between them the job might be accomplished. It seems reasonable to believe that He allows so many churches to reside in an area because He has a unique plan for each one; the plan is not for those bodies to be competitive but to be complementary in ministry. Each church has been called into existence to reach a different group of people and to have a unique influence on the culture in which it ministers.

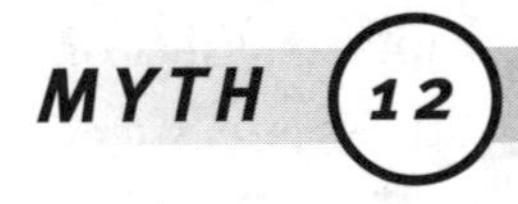

If it is truly God's vision for ministry, capturing that vision will be a simple, quick process.

REALITY

God's vision is not constrained by time.

In some cases, capturing God's vision for ministry requires the kind of intensive wrestling with God that characterized Jacob's wrestling match with God (see Gen. 32:22-32). In other situations, grasping the vision is more closely reflected by Paul's description of the long-distance race, which requires consistency and endurance over a prolonged period (see Phil. 3:13-14).

In certain cases, because of the constant brewing of God's vision in the heart of the leader, when that individual finally concentrates on clarifying and articulating the vision, it comes quickly. But there seems to be a consistent span of time during which God imparts His vision to people or during which visionary leaders are able to grasp that vision. The fact that a vision for ministry is determined in a short burst of energy is no more a sign that it is complete or from God than the assumption that one who has spent months seeking that vision has finally gleaned it. God's vision is not constrained by time; it is determined by our receptiveness and level of preparation to receive His insight.

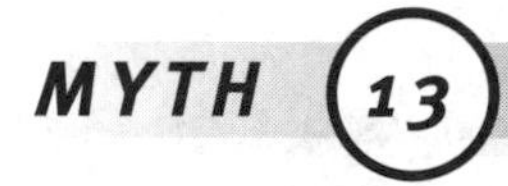

To develop vision, a pastor could identify several visionary business leaders and follow the same steps they had taken.

REALITY

Church leaders cannot blindly follow the path charted by people who operate on the basis of a different worldview.

Sadly, it seems true that you would more likely find visionary leaders in the business community than among the ranks of church leaders. However, there is some danger in following the paths charted by secular leaders when it comes to developing vision. First, business leaders seek to satisfy a different bottom-line objective (i.e., financial profits, not saved souls). Second, business leaders rely upon a different source for their guidance and insight (i.e., self, not God). While much understanding can be gained from studying the procedures and perspectives of visionary corporate leaders, church leaders should not blindly follow the path charted by people who operate on the basis of a different worldview or set of goals.

MYTH 14

Because vision is imparted by God to the pastor, other people have no role in the development of vision, only in its implementation.

REALITY

Other godly individuals are needed as a sounding board to evaluate the vision at various points in its development.

While God imparts the vision to the leader, He works through a variety of people and circumstances to enlarge the scope and perspective of the leader. People play a critical role in the development of vision, although it is not a committee-based activity. Other godly individuals are needed as a sounding board (e.g., counselors) to evaluate the vision at various points in its development. Other people can be instrumental in providing the pastor with important information to be used in gaining a context for understanding how God wants the church to move forward. The pastor is the point person and central figure in the process, but capturing God's vision for ministry is certainly not a solitary process.

MYTH 15

The best way to communicate vision is to develop a catchy slogan that people will remember.

REALITY

Too much emphasis upon a slogan can be detrimental.

A slogan is one means of effectively communicating the essence of the vision so that people have a shorthand way of recalling it. However, it is important not to confuse a slogan that encapsulates the heart of the vision with the actual vision itself. In many cases, slogans prove to be more harmful than useful because they trivialize the vision. Rather than capture the totality of the vision—in all its fullness, with all its nuances—some people focus solely upon the content communicated through the slogan and thus limit the potential of the ministry.

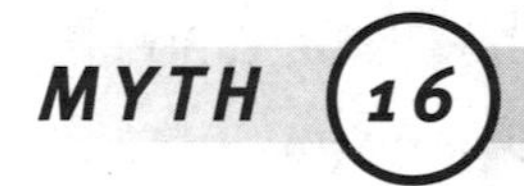

Sometimes God's vision for the future of a struggling congregation simply calls for the church to stabilize by maintaining its current position rather than to pursue growth aggressively.

REALITY

Encouraging people to pledge themselves to survival is an admission of defeat.

A declaration that admonishes people to hold the line as a means of facilitating effective ministry is not a vision statement but a death warrant. Vision is a creative, ongoing progress. It emphasizes aggressive futuristic thinking and action.

MYTH 17

If it takes too long to develop, the result probably is not true vision.

REALITY

God may take more pleasure in our attempt to know His mind than in our eventual ability to capture that insight.

God does not place timetables on how quickly He expects us to capture His vision. In fact, He may be more pleased with our attempt to know His mind than in our eventual ability to capture that insight. The key is that we develop a lifestyle characterized by the vision-capturing process—that is, a life in which He is preeminent, in which our desires are to know and please Him and our activities center around our relationship with Him. While time is of the essence because we do not know how long we have to reach a dying, sinful world with the gospel, we also know that He delights in the time we spend talking with Him and serving Him. Our only guarantee in the vision-development process is that He will impart His vision for our ministry to us. The guarantee does not come with a schedule attached.

MYTH 18

It is reasonable to expect a denomination to dictate the vision for ministry to each of its member churches, leaving the development of strategy and implementation up to the church's creative process.

REALITY

If a vision for individual churches is mandated from the denominational level, it assumes that the pastor of a church is not a leader but simply a manager.

This myth is a wholly unreasonable approach to capturing God's vision for ministry. The leader of a given denomination must possess God's vision for the ministry of the denomination. However, that vision will likely differ in significant ways from the grassroots realities of the vision for any given congregation. If a denomination were to mandate a vision for each church, this assumes that the pastor of a church is not truly a leader but simply a manager. It also assumes that God has somehow determined that each church in the denomination is facing identical societal circumstances and has equivalent material and human resources. God is certainly capable of doing that, but to my knowledge, such conditions have never actually existed. It is reasonable to expect a denomination to identify a broadly accepted statement of mission for ministry.

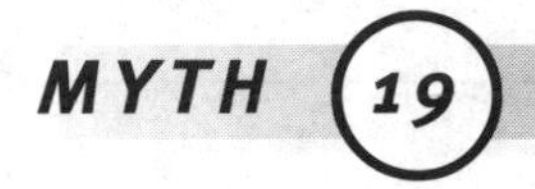

A church's vision needs to be re-created every couple of years.

REALITY

Vision usually outlasts the visionary.

Interestingly, when God imparts His vision for a church's ministry, the vision often outlasts the visionary. In other words, His vision is long lasting; it is not something that will change frequently. If a church were to change its vision every two or three years, the result would be constant chaos. As soon as the congregation reached a point at which people and systems were in place to make things happen in response to the vision, it would be time to turn things upside down again. Understand that the strategy and tactics related to the vision will change regularly, but the vision itself is not likely to shift much, if at all, over time.

MYTH 20

If a pastor simply loves the Lord and does the things described in the Bible as the qualities of a good leader—teaching, preaching, praying, modeling forgiveness and love and so forth—the church will grow, vision or no vision.

REALITY

Effective leaders must be visionaries.

The qualities outlined in passages such as 1 Timothy 3 and in Paul's epistle to Titus are absolutely necessary qualities for leaders. And so is God's vision for ministry. While the Bible never directly refers to this insight with the terminology we are using, it is packed with references and inferences to the necessity of operating on the basis of such insight. Consider, for example, the foundation for the words and actions in passages such as Psalm 32:8; Proverbs 3:5-6; 24:5-6 and 29:18; John 16:13-14; Romans 12:2; 2 Corinthians 12:1; Ephesians 5:17 and 6:6; and Colossians 1:9-10.

In the chapters that follow, we will examine in greater detail why the ideas labeled "myths" are nothing more than empty and misleading notions and how a pastor seeking to be a truly visionary leader serving God might address each of those erroneous perceptions.

Whose Vision Are You Following?

Chapter Highlights

- Man's vision for ministry is replete with limitations.
- God's vision is achieved through us but is not focused on us.
- God will bless and support His vision for your ministry.
- God's vision for your ministry is inspired.

Chapter 5

Whose Vision Are You Following?

I have learned a lot about vision by reading business books and journal articles that discuss the topic. Many of the authors demonstrate great wisdom in their writings about the importance, development and deployment of vision. Their work has undoubtedly helped many corporate executives refine their purpose in life as well as in the marketplace.

John Sculley, for example, rose to the top in his profession, becoming the youngest president ever appointed at PepsiCo. Soon after reaching that pinnacle, however, he left that company to become an executive at Apple Computer, Inc., where he was the CEO for a number of years.

Like many pastors who accept a position at a plateaued church, John Sculley joined Apple Computer, Inc., with limited resources.

Although he arrived in northern California to shepherd Apple with no background in technology or computers, Sculley was already recognized by his peers as a superb leader.

Vision is one of the keys to putting Sculley's success at Pepsi and at Apple into perspective. In his book *Odyssey*, Sculley credits his victories in business to a heightened emphasis upon vision.

> Traditional marketers are obsessed with the notion that marketing is a quantitative process. Successful marketing, however, cannot be merely reduced to a set of quantitative skills or measurements. While such skills may reduce the risks of making a big mistake, they are a poor substitute for true creative vision.[1]

Sculley admits that being a visionary leader is neither simple nor automatically accepted by those who must implement the vision. "It takes a passionate belief in the power of your own ideas and the conviction to see them through to the end. It can sometimes be a lonesome and long battle to win.

"Visionaries are constantly fighting conventional wisdom because they see the world ahead in terms of what it can be if someone is willing to look at things in very different ways."[2]

Sculley insists that vision is an all-encompassing passion about the challenges at hand. "Visionaries invest their lives in a product by becoming totally absorbed by every aspect of it."[3]

He also believes the reason many organizations lack vitality and impact is because they are led by individuals who see their role as that of competitor rather than as an innovator.

"Competitors believe that every battle counts, especially their most recent one, so they are too focused on the outcome of the month or the quarter. Visionaries are constantly looking over the horizon to tomorrow. If their vision is on target, they will change the market and they will prosper—even if it means losing a few battles along the way."[4]

Like many pastors who accept a position at a plateaued or declining church, Sculley entered Apple with great fanfare but with limited resources to make things happen. Undaunted, he took time to understand the market and the corporate culture. Ultimately, he realized that the key to success at Apple was restoring the vision.

> Turning the company around wasn't the difficult part. The hard part was knowing what to turn the company into. A tremendous amount of advice poured in from all quarters during the crisis. Most of it, in hindsight, was poor advice. We would have destroyed the company if we had followed most of it. Instead, we held close to our dream and vision.[5]

God, the Missing Link

While books by Sculley and other authors underscore the importance of vision in the business world, they fail to include an irreplaceable factor in the equation from a Christian perspective: the mind of God.

To typical business people, the ultimate corporate goal is to increase profits. To accomplish that goal, vision is an invaluable tool. It helps them imagine a better future and to foresee a means of creating that superior future reality. Given a studied grasp of existing conditions in the marketplace and a native talent for seizing untapped opportunities, a vision statement can be articulated that will lead to a better tomorrow. With that vision in mind, strategic initiatives can be created and implemented to bring about the desired outcome.

To corporate leaders who are responsible for creating the vision, the key resources in that process are the leaders themselves. Leaders study and analyze the marketplace to identify strengths and weaknesses, obstacles and opportunities. Leaders summon the insight, the courage and the tangible resources to create a brighter scenario for the future. Leaders set the goals and determine the means of satisfying those goals.

Vision Tension

Often, Christians who rise to executive positions in the business world find that they must wrestle with a tension between the corporate culture and their spiritual beliefs. The corporation emphasizes profits. The Christian faith emphasizes people. In the corporate structure, the CEO is the ultimate leader. In the Christian faith, God is the true leader. To nonbelievers who lead corporations, the wisdom that underlies the vision is innate. To Christians who serve God in the capacity of corporate executives, the wisdom to make it all happen comes from God. Reconciling these vastly divergent perspectives often becomes confusing to leaders and their followers as they attempt to make sense of these competing perspectives.

Yet, while tension may be created for a person who is a disciple of Christ and a business leader, the Bible is clear on how a Christian should behave in the marketplace. For Christians in a position of leadership, an entirely different set of values and goals must be embraced from those followed by individuals who have a philosophy not centered on knowing, loving and serving God. For Christians, leadership means more than simply having a strong bottom line: it means conducting all business endeavors in such a manner as to serve and bring glory to God. Because of this radically different set of values, Christian leaders also must have a different understanding of vision.

A vision that is not God centered may enjoy temporary success but probably will not provide a long-lasting impact.

Christian leaders must recognize that any vision based upon their own capacities will be flawed and limited. Because they are sinful individuals with restricted capacities and selfish tendencies, relying upon their own intuition, skills, talents, insights and dreams is dangerous, especially when the objective is to determine how to conduct effective ministry.

Authentic Christian leaders are people who know that when they are left alone to make decisions, those choices invariably reflect their unregenerate nature. In other words, their choices demonstrate values, beliefs, desires and goals that are not perfectly aligned with the mind and heart of God. But because they are Christian leaders, they know they must pursue God to gain a better perspective on what they ought to do with the resources and opportunities entrusted to them by God.

Man's Vision Flawed

When people create a vision that is not God centered, it may result in temporal progress but unlikely will provide a positive, long-lasting impact.

In fact, when we rely upon our own faculties to create a vision for the future, God is probably shaking His head in disappointment. "The Lord knows the thoughts of man; he knows that they are futile" (Ps. 94:11). Because we know that we are engaged in a battle between more than just flesh and blood, but in a battle of the principalities (see Eph. 6:12), we must do what we can to lean on the wisdom, insights and knowledge of the One who has the big picture and all its details in full view and who will lead us with our own best interests in mind.

All you have to do is examine the visions of men who are considered leaders by the world to see the absolute futility of man's best efforts without the special anointing and guidance of God.

If you study the vision espoused by many of today's leading business executives, you will find that their vision rarely reflects a desire to glorify the Creator who allowed them to rise to their leadership post. Their vision generally has little to do with the advancement of society and the restoration of a God-fearing culture or righteous values. Their vision statements generally focus upon profitability, organizational expansion, image enhancement, product improvement or creative initiative. These are not, in themselves, improper ends to pursue. They do, however, reflect the limitations of man-centered vision.

Those visions reek of egocentricity. Their underlying belief is that we will achieve our objectives if we simply try hard enough, if we are clever enough, if we employ sophisticated techniques or if we deftly use the world to our advantage. The only thing standing between us and total satisfaction, in this view, is our own ineptitude. We ought to be capable of achieving whatever we set our minds on doing.

The Limitations of Man's Vision

Visions created by men are, nevertheless, tempered by their perceptions of human limitations, resource realities and incomplete information about the environments they seek to conquer. While individuals may dream big, they also will dream realistically. Believing that they cannot defy the laws of science, dismiss the lessons of history or expand the natural abilities of people and organizations, such visions are restrained by known or assumed limitations of natural, physical, emotional, financial and legal realities.

Those visions also are based upon the ability of the human mind to conceive a grand plan. Without supernatural intervention, we cannot dream any bigger than our imagination will allow. Our imagination is limited by the raw data (i.e., the informational building blocks) that we have encountered and have intellectually or emotionally processed. And we rarely dare to plan for that which we cannot expect to become reality.

Put all of these factors together and you realize the vision developed by human beings suffers from tremendous limitations. The vision is limited by personal abilities and capabilities. It is filtered through societal and cultural boundaries and expectations. It is hindered by organizational restrictions and obstacles. It is sometimes constrained by communal bonds. And it usually is limited in a serious way by the absence of a spiritual perspective built in to the fabric of the inputs and the process.

The most successful individual has strong reason to ignore personal abilities and instead turn to God for vision.

Because of these restrictions, man's vision for the future is relatively predictable and mundane. Granted, a good vision that is well articulated is sometimes capable of stimulating creative and superior performance. People's vision rarely reaches the pinnacle, though, because it has been fathered by a limited source. In fact, the vision developed by people runs the risk of being the wrong vision for a group of people at a given time in history. Because the vision was developed in the wake of an information base, a psychological filter and a creative process flooded with imperfections, the statistical probability of the vision being imperfect is enormously high.

Thus, even when we put our most intelligent and skilled people in the role of the visionary, their chances of producing a perfect vision for the organization are slim.

An Unlimited Resource

By definition, that which God produces is perfect. And one of the resources He continues to produce today is a vision for His people to embrace and pursue.

God retains a call on everyone's life and ministry. While we have the ability to accept or reject that calling, He makes an understanding of the vision for our future available if we diligently seek it.

Even the most successful and self-absorbed individual has strong reason to ignore personal abilities and instead turn to God for vision.

Perfect

First, His vision for your ministry is perfect. It is the most appropriate vision for you given your situation. It reflects a perfect knowledge of all circumstances and a perfect understanding of all potential and possibilities. It is the vision that perfectly corresponds to His plan for the world and to your best interests. It also is a vision that you can readily accomplish through His desire and His power. No plan can humanly be conceived that can outshine the one He has divinely created for you.

Blessed

Second, He will bless His vision for your ministry. He is bound to support what He has conceived and imparted to His chosen leaders. It would be outside the boundaries of God's character to conceive the vision, to implant it in the minds and hearts of His people and then to turn His back on them as they seek to be faithful to the vision. His record, through the actions of David, Nehemiah, Paul and others, clearly shows how consistent He will be with His vision for us. He will bless it because the vision fulfilled will bring Him honor, glory and joy. His vision is a fail-safe strategy for people to pursue.

Inspired

Third, God's vision for your ministry is inspired. Because it was conceived by the God who created all things from nothing and who controls the world in eternity, His vision is bigger than anything we could create. Consequently, when you grasp His vision for your ministry, it will be exciting to behold. Indeed, embracing and carrying out that vision will bring you unimaginable gratification and fulfillment.

When you capture His vision for your ministry, you will find that it has God at the center. His vision is based on the values and principles that are central to His Word and reflect His character. His vision is achieved through us but is not focused on us. While the vision may entail actions we take for the good of other people, the ultimate end is to please and exalt the Lord.

While the visions detailed by leaders of business and government institutions may encompass a variety of goals, the vision of God imparted to a true leader invariably has but one goal: glorifying Him by building His kingdom. There may be a variety of paths toward the achievement of that goal, but the goal itself is always the same.

Trial by Fire

Make no mistake about it, grasping God's vision for your ministry is not a simple task. But it is a necessary endeavor.

Consider this: All leaders, regardless of their abilities and their relationship with God, encounter crises. Even in a setting of Christian service, leaders encounter difficulties. Realize that a crisis is not necessarily a negative situation. A crisis is simply a turning point at which your ability to lead is tested. In the days ahead, you can count on being confronted by some type of crisis.

If you are truly a godly leader pursuing His vision, it is probable that when you next encounter a crisis that threatens the progress and impact of your work, you will succeed and move on to even greater challenges. If you are not truly seeking to build His kingdom but to build something or somebody else, you probably will fail and will have to regroup.

For many people, it is during times of crisis that the value of having God's vision is most obvious. It provides strength, direction, motivation and peace. And trying to lead people without such a vision merely hastens the coming of a crisis. And then another. And another. Trying to master a crisis situation successfully without true vision is like trying to write a book without having a means of recording your thoughts. You simply do not have the tools to accomplish the task.

The situation boils down to this: In a time of crisis, whose vision would you rather rely upon, yours or God's? Yours could be sufficiently strong to get by, or it could be wholly inadequate and could result in abysmal failure. Alternatively, you could recognize that God's vision cannot be wrong. His vision for your ministry will be perfect, appropriate, blessed, achievable and satisfying.

You can be assured that crises, trials and tests will come your way. If you have decided to trust God for your eternal future, it is just as reasonable for you to entrust your temporal future to Him as well.

Notes

1. John Sculley, *Odyssey* (New York: HarperCollins, 1987), p. 23.
2. Ibid.
3. Ibid., p. 24.
4. Ibid., p. 262.
5. Ibid., p. 263.

Capturing God's Vision

Chapter Highlights

- Know yourself.
- Know your ministry environment.
- Know God.
- Know objective wisdom.

Chapter 6

Capturing God's Vision

Questions nagged at two men. The first wanted to serve God but didn't like the church. The second served a church but didn't like the ministry.

"Having a strong sense of wanting to do good work or to be effective in ministry isn't enough," the first man says today. "You've got to develop and fine-tune that vision for ministry before you can hope to get people on board and to have ministry take off."

His initial dislike for the church later served as the framework upon which God built his ministry. After praying faithfully every day and "practically screaming at God" for an answer, he found that God was calling him to develop a church for those who hate church.

"The amazing thing about the vision He gave me is that it has instilled excitement in me and in others to do something that we ordinarily might not be the least bit excited about. When I speak to pastors, I tell them right off: Don't even attempt to do ministry until vision is in place."

The second pastor became restless after serving a traditional, mainline church for several years. The church was growing; he and his family enjoyed the community; and his ministry was considered successful. However, deep inside, he felt dissatisfied and unfulfilled.

"If you don't think that my feeling disenchanted with a viable church situation didn't raise a ton of guilt, think again," he says. "How could a man of God be so blessed and feel so unfulfilled? I didn't share those feelings with anyone, even my wife, for the longest time. I just kept trying to shove the feelings down and kept doing what I must have been called to do. After all, I was a minister of the gospel. What nobler calling could a man have?

"But I couldn't keep it up. Finally, I realized, *Hey, wait a minute, maybe that's God's way of getting my attention and telling me He has something else in store for me.* Once I realized that and opened my eyes to it, a huge burden lifted."

At that point, he turned to the tools of the trade: praying, reading Scripture and talking with colleagues. "I realized that I'd burned out on my own and it was time to rely on Him for direction. So I entered a time of real soul-searching and tried to get a handle on what God was trying to get me to do. Today, of course, I know that He wanted me to minister on the basis of vision, not just tradition and training."

It took several months to clarify the vision in his mind and heart. "I knew it had to do with church and reaching lost people," he says. "That's just how He wired me. But I already was in a church and already had a passion to reach lost people. I knew He had something deeper in mind, something that would stretch me more and would reap greater fruit."

After an extensive search, the man realized that God was leading him to a different place, to a different style of ministry and to a different type of people.

"It was scary and exciting at the same time," he says. "That vision has proved to be absolutely the best thing that could have happened for me. At the time I was excited, but not without some reservations about the magnitude of the task. It just seemed awesome compared to who I was. So I figured, *Hey, it's His vision; I'm His man; let Him work through me;* and He has."

The vision led this pastor and his family to move to another state and to plant a church whose membership has mushroomed from 25 to more than 1,500 people in 6 years.

"One of the chief lessons for me was discovering the difference between doing what people expect a pastor to do and doing what God has called me to do," he says. "In my previous position I was carrying the mission without vision. Now, I'm pursuing the vision within the context of our mission to serve God.

"As a church, we're more focused, more together, more purposeful, because we have a common goal and a unique vision of why God has us here. We don't do church just because that's the thing to do. We're alive in our faith and ministry because of a special call He gave to the people, through me, to be His church."

An Investment in Vision

If you, like those two pastors, wish to grasp the vision for ministry He has in mind for you, plan to make an investment in that process.

If you were to develop a strategic plan, you could imitate some of the strategies and tactics used by other organizations that sought to achieve a similar outcome as yours. If you were to motivate people to participate in a ministry opportunity, you could study how other churches had stimulated people to action and adapt their methods. If you were to seek money for a new building program, you could evaluate fund-raising techniques used in other communities and borrow principles from those experiences.

If you wish to grasp God's vision for ministry, plan to make an investment in that process.

But when it comes to vision, you cannot simply examine the vision statements of other churches and say to yourself, *That looks great; I'd love to do that; let's embrace that as our vision.* If you are truly seeking God's vision for your ministry, it is a personal matter between you and Him. To understand fully the vision, you must be prepared to invest yourself in the acquisition process. His vision, however, does not come without cost.

The Components of Vision

In seeking His vision, you must address four crucial components. Having insight into any one of those areas is in itself insufficient. As Paul wrote, "Do not deceive yourselves. If any one of you thinks he is wise by the standards of this age, he should become a 'fool' so that he may become wise. For the wisdom of this world is foolishness in God's sight" (1 Cor. 3:18-19).

What principles, then, do you need to grasp in order to acquire His vision for your ministry? First, you must know yourself. Second, you must know the ministry environment in which you reside. Third, you must know God intimately. Fourth, you must gain objective wisdom related to your search.

What you can know ahead of time is that God has prepared you for a special ministry. He is willing to impart to you the big picture and the details of that ministry if you are serious about perceiving, embracing and pursuing your life's purpose. His vision for you is a precious commodity that only He can impart. It is a gift that must be desired if He is to bestow it upon you. It is not a gift without a price tag. He gives it with the expectation that you will commit your life to fulfilling that vision. A lesser commitment to the acquisition of the vision will result in a ministry that fails to understand or realize its potential.

COMPONENT 

Know Yourself

Much of the process of capturing His vision for your ministry relates to the refinement of knowledge. As the writer of Proverbs points out, "Every prudent man acts out of knowledge, but a fool exposes his folly" (Prov. 13:16). One of the most important types of knowledge you can possess is knowledge about yourself: how He has created you and how you perceive the world in light of your abilities and character.

God is not about to send you into battles on His behalf that you cannot win. But before you can emerge victorious from the various battlefields on which ministry takes place, you must have a concrete and accurate comprehension of who you are, how you have been gifted and the nature of your heart. Without such insight, the chances of your being able to comprehend fully the scope and detail of His vision are slight.

Start at the Beginning

To get to the point where He can entrust His gift of vision to you, begin by asking yourself why you are in ministry. Strip away all the seminary-taught answers and the socially acceptable responses. Go one-on-one with God and honestly tell Him why you are in ministry. What is your motivation?

I know a few individuals whose search for His vision ended at this early juncture. Upon coming clean before Him, they realized that their motives disqualified them from true leadership. They were out for applause and acceptance by the masses, power over people and organizations, the image of spirituality or being viewed as an expert. Their condition brought to mind the proverb that reads, "A fool finds no pleasure in understanding but delights in airing his own opinions" (Prov. 18:2).

How wonderful it is that these people were able to arrive at an honest assessment of who they were and why they were engaged in ministry. While the consequence of that honesty was painful, it was not as painful as a continued life of self-deception would have been. In the end, leaving full-time ministry for a period was preferable to leading hundreds of people into chaos and frustration because those pastors were playing a role they could not fill.

Ask Tough Questions

You must identify the values, attitudes, assumptions and experiences that undergird your ministry. It is not possible for a person to have complete self-knowledge unless some of these tough questions are faced.

You must identify the values, attitudes, assumptions and experiences that undergird your ministry.

One of the most revealing questions to ask is the identity of those matters about which you are passionate. What is it that, without fail, excites you in ministry? What are the ministry matters that keep you up late at night, dreaming with anticipation and expectation? What ministry outcomes do you personally yearn for? Because vision is effective only when there is passion behind the delivery, knowing those "passion points" is important.

In your self-evaluation you should also explore your understanding of personal strengths and weaknesses. In your effort to paint a realistic portrait of who you are, you must describe both sides of the fence—the good and the bad. Be as broad based in this examination as possible, looking not only at ministry-related qualities but also at your emotional, intellectual, interpersonal and physical characteristics.

What follows are some of the questions that have proven to be helpful to Christian leaders as they think through who they are and why they are involved in ministry.

Questions About Your Emotions

- What turns you on in life? What turns you off emotionally?
- During what situations do you feel most alive or exuberant?
- Which Bible figures capture your imagination? Why?
- What makes life worth living?
- Who are the three most important people in your life? Why?
- Who are the three people you most respect? Why?
- What is your personality type? How does that impact your ministry?

Questions About Your Abilities

- What are your spiritual gifts?
- What goals have you set and reached during the past five years?
- What goals have you set and failed to achieve during that period? What kept you from meeting your goals?
- What goals are you afraid to set because you feel incapable of reaching them?
- In what ways did God make you different from others? What unique or special talents do you possess?

Questions About Your Intellect and Perspectives

- How would you define a successful church? What would it take for your church to be successful?

- How would you define a successful pastor? What would it take for you to be successful?
- How would you define a godly Christian leader? How well do you fit that description?
- What differentiates a Christian leader from a non-Christian leader?
- Are you wise enough to discern His vision for your ministry?

Questions About Your Heart

- What makes you cry? Why?
- If you could accomplish only one task in life, what would it be? (Be honest on this one!)
- If your friends and family remembered only one thing about you after you died, what would you want them to remember?
- For what opportunities or outcomes would you be willing to endure physical persecution? Intellectual or emotional persecution?
- Which passages of the Bible speak most loudly and consistently to you?
- What sins do you commit most often?
- How deep is your relationship with God right now? What has the growth curve of your relationship with Him been over the past year?
- What activities do you get totally absorbed in? What activities are you unlikely to grow out of as you mature?
- What are the five values of human character to which you feel you must at all times, at all costs, be true?
- What characteristics are you committed to perfecting in your life?

Questions About Your Mentors and Models

- Who are the five spiritual leaders whom you have known personally and would most like to imitate? Why?
- Who have been the five most influential spiritual leaders in your life other than Jesus? Why?

- Other than spiritual mentors, who has influenced your life the most? How did they influence you? What gave them that influence?
- How do you differ from other pastors you know?
- What are the characteristics of an ideal pastor? Which of those do you possess? Which ones do you not possess?

Questions About Your Ministry

- Are you currently ministering on the basis of vision? If so, whose vision is it? How did you acquire that vision?
- What is your toughest duty or responsibility as a pastor?
- Which ministry activities make you depressed? Which ones make you most ambivalent? Which ones turn you off?
- What is your vision for your personal ministry; that is, the vision for your ministry apart from what you do as pastor of the church?
- Which people groups do you feel naturally drawn to in ministry?
- What makes full-time ministry worthwhile to you?
- Which ministry experiences have provided you with the greatest fulfillment? Which experiences produced the greatest disappointment?
- What is the role of your family in light of your ministry obligations?

Understand that these questions do not form an exhaustive list but are designed to get you thinking in areas that must be examined if you are to be prepared for God's vision for your ministry. He wants to use you in a special way. But you must be a leader committed to knowing and serving Him, which mandates having a firm and accurate understanding of your character, capabilities and heart.

COMPONENT 2

Know Your Ministry Environment

Good decisions are made in context. Therefore, it is important for you to obtain a realistic view of the context within which you will minister. If you are to receive accurately the vision He seeks to communicate to you, knowing the contours of the environment in which you will minister is an integral element that will help shape your understanding of what He is telling you.

Four dominant elements are involved in becoming acquainted with your ministry environment: your community, your colleagues, your congregation and your competition.

Your Community

It is important to have a working knowledge of the people who live in your geographic market. This marketplace may range from an established, easily identifiable rural community to a complex melting pot of cultures residing in a rapidly changing metropolitan area.

It is important to have a working knowledge of the people who live in your geographic market.

Among the pieces of information you should have at hand are the demographic attributes of the population, the key attitudes they possess, the values that determine their thoughts and lifestyles, the beliefs that shape their character, the lifestyles that describe their daily activities and the felt needs they possess.

This is an area in which a senior pastor can invite help from members of the congregation. This type of information is often used by marketing specialists, advertisers, social scientists and similar researchers and may be readily available through a single source, even a member of the congregation who works in one of these areas.

Personal conversations with the movers and shakers and opinion makers in the community add a human dimension to such a study. Talk with people like the police chief, the superintendent of schools, a municipal judge and the mayor. Don't overlook learning about the community through the eyes of other individuals who live, work and play in your community.

Your Colleagues

You should enjoy more than a "Hello, how are you?" relationship with other pastors of the gospel. After all, you are not in competition with them.

Part of your vision-capturing process is to understand why God has allowed other churches to exist in your area. My perspective is that He has gifted different churches in different ways to accomplish different tasks—tasks that may share a common mission but which do not conflict in terms of the audiences reached.

Interact with fellow pastors to discover their vision for ministry: how it is unique, what makes it distinctive, how it might complement what you might do, how you could support their efforts.

You also can learn from their experiences in the community and thereby avoid duplicating mistakes or pursuing unwise strategies. Their experiences may help you understand what God is leading you to do by providing a broader or deeper perspective on the parameters of ministry in your locale.

Your Congregation

To lead a group of people effectively, you must interpret the vision in a way that makes sense to them. In a church context, this means knowing the history of the congregation and having an accurate sense of the thinking and emotions of the people.

Talk with the people of your congregation to determine their frustrations with the church and its role in the community. Build significant relationships with people so that they can share honest feedback about the direction and future of the church. It would be advantageous to bounce ideas off people who demonstrate a keen interest in knowing where the church is going.

While they cannot dictate that vision for you, they can help you understand how the vision will impact the church, whether the vision seems truly appropriate for the church (or whether perhaps you have misread God's leading) and how you might best articulate the vision for those who must own and live it.

Your Competition

What is your competition? It is not the other churches in the area. Your competition is television, sleeping late, sales at the mall, local sports leagues or athletic opportunities, family activities, personal hobbies and similar events.

To make the most of God's vision for your ministry, have a firm grip on this competition and why people choose those options over involvement with the church. Also study the intensity of your community's commitment to those competitors. The answers to these questions will help you create a vision for ministry.

Know God

This may come across as a simplistic suggestion, a reality assumed to be a given for people who lead churches or who are involved in full-time ministry. Nevertheless, I am astonished at how many leaders spend little time regularly building their relationship with God and attempting to establish an ever-expanding knowledge of who He is.

Visionary Christian leaders have made it plain to me that you cannot know His vision for your ministry unless you first know God. That knowledge must transcend simply acknowledging Christ as Lord and Savior or consenting that God is eternal, perfect and omnipotent. The relationship must be deep and personal. And the chances are good that unless you know Him to that degree, He will have little interest in divulging that vision to you because He is not a high enough priority in your life for you to seek an evolving relationship.

Visionary Christian leaders have made it plain that you cannot know God's vision for your ministry unless you first know God.

Let me recommend three critical means to knowing Him in preparation for the communication of vision.

Study the Word

First, study the Bible. Get beyond reading it merely for the sake of being in the Word. Move past the point of regarding the Bible as a resource upon which you build sermons or teaching. Treat the Bible as the sacred text that it is, one that unlocks the mysteries of His nature, the fullness of His dreams, the wisdom of His methods.

The Bible should serve as a means of fortifying the relationship you wish to build with God. If fear of the Lord is the beginning of wisdom, get to know Him so well that you have that balance between the healthy fear of an all-powerful, ruling Creator and a sense of closeness with a loving, forgiving Father.

Keep in mind that you are trying to figure out how God has used and worked through other people of limited intellect and natural talents in leading them to a vision that was clearly bigger than they were or something that they could not have developed in and of themselves. Understanding how God has worked in the lives of other visionaries will clarify for you some of the ways that He works in our lives today.

Follow the activities and the lines of reasoning ascribed to Paul. Put yourself in David's place and comprehend his circumstances and his heart. Evaluate the decisions of Joshua and how his relationship with God shaped his determinations. Gain invaluable insights into the ways in which these role models lived, prayed, worshiped and used the spiritual disciplines.

You also will become better acquainted with the characteristics and attributes of God. As you draft a vision statement, this study might prompt you to say: "Hey, wait a minute, I know that God has *A, B* and *C* attributes. I know His characteristics are *X, Y* and *Z.* This kind of vision doesn't seem to come from God because it is inconsistent with who I know Him to be."

The study also will affect your heart, your attempt to figure out who you are in light of who He is. You may ask such questions as: What is my heart? What am I trying to accomplish? Am I trying to use God for my benefit?

In determining the appropriate condition of your heart, review the ultimate example of Jesus Christ, the lives of other visionaries and how God Himself talked to His creation and worked through it in very tangible and specific ways. Until your heart is in the right place, the possibility of God giving and entrusting His vision to you are relatively slim. The resource is too precious to be shared randomly.

Imagine the book that could be written about your life as a person after God's own heart, entrusted by God Himself with a personal, custom-made vision for ministry and how adequately you lived that vision. How would you like that book to read?

Your exploration of the Bible will likely fuel your intellectual ability to relate to God.

Reassess Your Prayer Life

Study of the Word and prayer are a unified process. However, you can fuel your relationship with God by praying to Him. In grasping vision, prayer is an indispensable ingredient in the process.

Typically, prayer is a kind of request line where we ask God for those things that are pleasing to us as opposed to letting Him know our condition and our availability to serve Him. We are going to make bold requests, but the thing that should motivate our requests is an understanding of how He can use us in a particular set of circumstances to achieve specific outcomes. The key is not so much what we want to accomplish but that we are willing vessels awaiting His direction on how we can be more useful to Him in ministry.

In vision development, prayer is critical because it is a time when you can ask God to speak to you. He may do so by conveying impressions that you must then pursue in more tangible terms. He may do so by speaking directly to you in words that seem audible. The key is to be silent and focused enough to allow Him to break through to you and to communicate what He wants you to grasp.

American church leaders generally feel they are successful only when they are active.

A vital part of knowing His vision is to be still and attentive long enough to hear Him. The leaders of American Christian churches are generally people who feel they are successful only when they are active. God, however, seems to speak most clearly to Christian leaders when they are inactive; that is, when they have made a conscious effort to allow Him to lead the conversation and to impart wisdom in His own way, in His own timing. This requires you to spend much time allowing Him to direct your thoughts. The unsettling part of this process is that you must clearly allow Him to be in control. That is a tough reality for many leaders to accept.

During those prayer times when you are imparting your requests, be sure to ask Him to prepare you for the vision and to communicate to you with clarity. When you believe you have heard and understood that vision, be sure to ask Him to bless it to His glory.

Practice Fasting

A third means of facilitating your knowledge of God is through fasting. In the sense that the Bible is old-fashioned, you could argue that fasting is, too. This discipline, however, was invaluable for helping Nehemiah,

David, Paul and other visionaries in the Bible draw closer to God and to concentrate on His guidance, and it is one of the basic disciplines that God wants leaders to practice today. Again, it is a reflection of where your heart is. It is not so much a means of cleansing as it is of preparation so that God can really reach you. There is nothing magic about fasting. It is a part of the process of preparing for your vision-grasping journey.

COMPONENT 4

Verify the Vision

"Where there is no counsel, the people fall; but in the multitude of counselors there is safety" (Prov. 11:14, *NKJV*).

Certainly it is a valuable experience to be surrounded by those who care about you and your ministries and who are wise in the ways of the Lord. One of the greatest values they bring to your life is their ability to speak honestly and openly regarding your efforts to serve God. In like manner, how fruitful it is to have those people offer their perceptions regarding your ideas on God's vision for your ministry.

The purpose of gaining the perspective of outside counselors is not to allow them to determine or to frame the vision. Rather, they can help you be as certain as possible that you have truly grasped the vision God has prepared for you and have not succumbed to the desire to follow the ways that seem right to you alone. Knowing that vision requires change, hard work, commitment and perseverance, you will be tempted to temper your perception of God's vision with a softer edge. The wisdom of counselors often challenges that softening, bringing you back to a more complete understanding of God's desire for you and your church.

In reviewing your perception of God's vision for ministry, you must be totally honest and open about that vision. Allow your counselors to respond after a full disclosure of your understanding of the vision and your reaction to it. Pray with those individuals that they, too, might share in the peace of God regarding that vision.

Don't Be Discouraged

One of the more difficult tasks in the vision adventure is to hear your trusted advisers tell you that your journey of discovery appears to be incomplete or that you must continue to pursue God for a deeper understanding. Do not deal with such advice as failure but rather as an indication that the process was interrupted prematurely. In the end, your ministry will be better off for the perseverance of seeking clarification and expansion of the vision.

Your advisers may not have the depth of insight about the vision that you possess. That is only natural given the substantial investment you have made in the process. However, do not be too quick to discount the words of those who are being used by God to sharpen your perspective. "The way of a fool seems right to him, but a wise man listens to advice" (Prov. 12:15).

When Will You Have God's Vision?

There is no way of telling how long it will take you to grasp God's vision for your ministry. Some leaders say that it took them just a few days. Others confide that it took them many months to gain clarity on the issue. Some pastors I have spoken with express disbelief that it might take a true leader so long to capture the mind of God in this area. Realize, however, that not every leader has been trained to think along the lines of knowing and leaning upon God's vision. The individuals who spent months and months seeking His direction were those who were honest enough to admit that either they were out of touch with Him, that they needed to realign their hearts to be pure enough to hear Him or that they had never truly served on the basis of His vision but had been pursuing their own. You also may discover that you are not a leader and therefore have no vision. People who are managers and not leaders can work a lifetime on a vision statement and not determine God's calling for their church.

The most important factor is to pursue His vision doggedly. Do not let the wear and tear of the process defeat you. It takes time. It takes intellectual and emotional effort. It takes a willingness to be vulnerable with counselors. It takes digging deep inside yourself to be vulnerable before God. We live in a society that denigrates such efforts. You may minister in a church where most people would not understand the depth of commitment that vision requires or where the lay leaders are impatient to initiate a vision statement. What matters is how you commit yourself to Him, to His guidance and to being faithful to carry out the vision He has prepared for you.

7

The Character of God's Vision

Chapter Highlights

- When you capture God's vision for your ministry, it will have specific, predictable qualities.
- God's vision is inspiring.
- Vision is a means of describing the activity and development of the ministry.
- God's vision for you will cause you to go beyond the limitations you assumed were obstacles.
- Vision is empowering.
- God has created a personal vision that fits you perfectly.
- Vision is detailed.
- Vision is people oriented.

Chapter 7
The Character of God's Vision

Earlier, I indicated that definitions of vision somehow do not do justice to the real thing. Such descriptions seem a bit removed from the heartbeat of true vision. The definitions provided in the earlier portions of this text serve only as a useful guide to working through the process and arriving at God's view of what you could best be doing to please Him.

In the next few pages, perhaps we can build on the definition and make the process come alive. As you begin to grasp the dimensions and body of the vision, you will discover that it begins to change who you are. Because the vision becomes the driving force in your sense of purpose, it reshapes your personality and your behavior to a significant degree.

The Characteristics of Vision

To make the most of your time spent learning about yourself, about God and about His desires for your ministry, it might be productive to consider some of the likely characteristics of the vision itself because those traits will alter your perspectives and actions.

Realize that your vision will reflect your most basic values and beliefs. Those elements are an inseparable part of you, and they become integrated into every decision and judgment you make. They also are important because they serve as part of the filter through which you determine how to respond to the ever-changing circumstances. This is one of the reasons why it is important that vision, as opposed to mission, be specific and detailed.

While you may not have a well-defined, clearly articulated philosophy of life or philosophy of ministry, your vision acts as a default mechanism that enables you to make consistent decisions in the absence of such a philosophy. In the meantime, we can examine more closely the following attributes of the vision God has prepared for you.

Vision Is Inspiring

Can you imagine understanding God's perspective of the world and how He wishes to use you in shaping that world and then feeling let down by His viewpoint? Hardly! What could be more inspiring than pursuing the dreams that He has for your life? When you obtain His vision for your ministry, you will undoubtedly be excited and stimulated to get on with the work at hand.

In speaking with pastors who have worked through the vision-capturing process and are now working at implementing the vision, several stated that they believe there is a distinct difference between the process of capturing and the experience of living the vision. For these men, the process was like an intensive counseling experience. The process began to have impact only when they reached the point at which they were committed to making it work. It took hours of reflection, study, prayer and interaction, resulting in incremental progress toward discovering the vision.

When the vision was etched upon their hearts, though, entirely different procedures were put into place, and a gamut of disparate emotions emerged. From their descriptions, it seems that the process was intimate, delicate and exhausting. It was filled with the wonder of mystery and discovery and brought them through the highs and lows of revelation about self, the world, other people and their faith-based relationship with the Trinity. The vision-implementation process, in contrast, was an energizing, motivating, exciting endeavor. It has its moments of frustration based on the inability to realize the desired outcomes or the agonizingly slow pace of progress. But the ability to foresee the outcome and to believe that God will bless efforts toward that outcome permits the leader to maintain enthusiasm and excitement about the journey.

Most of the leaders interviewed agreed that vision itself is probably not from God if it does not excite you to the point that you occasionally find yourself being impatient with people, systems and situations. The visionary pastors also noted that they sometimes reach a state of euphoria about the prospects that may result from the vision. This, in itself, was a new experience for some of these men because they were not particularly emotional beings. Yet, the force of the vision was something that caused them to overflow with feeling about the potential and the impact of having the vision become a reality.

Vision, then, becomes a bold reason for living. It is a badge of purpose that the bearer wears proudly and courageously. Vision is not vision if it is not inspiring.

Vision Is Change Oriented

Science has taught us that every living entity is constantly changing. Scientists have even agreed upon a term to describe those entities that are not undergoing constant change. That term is "dead." Likewise, a ministry that aims for something other than change invites euthanasia.

Vision is a means of describing the activity and development of the ministry, the way in which the ministry will become more significant in the lives of people. A vision from God goes beyond the simple recognition that change is healthy; it celebrates the ability and opportunity to change.

Vision becomes a bold reason for living. It is a badge of purpose that the bearer wears proudly and courageously.

You may wonder why God would not instill within us a vision for the status quo. Think about organizations, people or movements that strive to maintain the same set of activities and performance level over time. They lack excitement. They are incapable of inspiring and activating people. They fail to have a growing (or, perhaps, any) impact on society. In fact, because the rest of the world is making progress and seeking to grow, the status quo group actually loses ground by seeking to remain in the same place.

Our God is not One who is satisfied with routine and blandness. He is the God of creativity and diversity, a Creator responsible for progress and advancement (see Ps. 104:1-13). He could easily have created a world in which change was foreign or despised. Instead, He introduced change and used it as a means of making His creation more interesting and lovable. So should we, His Church, invest our energies into seeking positive change for the growth of His people and the building of His kingdom.

Vision Is Challenging

God loves to stretch His people. His vision for your ministry will do just that. Rest assured that His vision for you will cause you to do things you have never done before, to exceed the barriers you assumed were impenetrable obstacles.

In a secularized culture like ours, simply knowing, loving and serving God is a challenge. But to do so in a ground-breaking, life-changing, effective way is an even more daunting task. While we may approach the implementation of the vision as something to be accomplished through a series of incremental gains, remember that the vision itself will be large enough in scope that we will find ourselves consistently straining to develop new ideas and new approaches to achieve the desired ends.

And that is partially what makes real ministry so riveting and encompassing: the challenge of making the seemingly impossible possible.

Vision Is Empowering

This is one of the key differences between a vision for ministry and a vision for business. In ministry, vision empowers people to serve others, ultimately serving God in the process. In business, the vision frequently explores ways of expanding the corporation by enabling others to serve the needs of the corporation. Worldly vision is inward focused; God's vision for ministry is outward focused.

As you examine the character of the vision for ministry to which you cling, ask yourself this: When you read the vision statement or describe the vision for newcomers, do they perceive the vision as one that prepares and requires them to serve other people or as one that indicates they will be served by the church? If it is the latter, either the description lacks clarity, or the vision itself is not truly from God.

Vision Is Long-Term

God's vision for your ministry will not change quickly, nor will it be something you will accomplish rapidly. His vision will require years of active pursuit. The vision itself may outlive you.

Thus, the heart of the vision will remain unchanged over a prolonged period. Some of the details lying at the outer edge of your understanding of the vision may shift somewhat over the course of time. But the core of the vision—the people you have been called to reach, the task you have been called to do, the purpose for which you exist—will remain constant. Because He is not a God of confusion but of order, because He is a God who is in control, because He takes great pleasure in seeing us find success in our service, He will be faithful in His support of the vision.

God's vision for your ministry will not change quickly, nor will it be something you will accomplish rapidly. But it may outlive you.

The implication of this reality is that your vision will not change every year or two. You do not need to ponder constantly whether you are pursuing the right vision for the near future. Your energy ought to be dedicated to doing the ministry He has outlined for you as distilled within the vision.

Vision Is Customized

Your God is a personal God. He carefully created you. He knows you intimately. He wants to have a growing relationship with you. He, therefore, has created a personalized vision that fits you perfectly.

What a mess the world would be if God took a mechanical approach to His people. Imagine Him saying, "Here's a pretty good generic vision, a one-size-fits-all vision. When My people seek My face and My mind, I will simply lead them to this predictable but viable vision. Let them figure out how to avoid overlap and confusion. If they're clever enough, it will all work out in the end."

No, your God is so personally involved with you that He has created a customized vision for you and you alone. The vision is unique to your circumstances and calibrated to your abilities. Why would He bother? Because God is your partner in ministry. What kind of relationship would it be if He dictated the rules of the game and then simply watched you wallow in your ineptitude and confusion as you tried to put the pieces together and make ministry happen apart from His power and guidance?

You cannot copy the vision of another church or another pastor. If they have done their homework and worked on their relationship with God properly, their vision is unique to who they are and to what God has designed them to accomplish for the Kingdom. Similarly, you need not be protective of your vision because it is relevant only to your ministry.

Vision Is Detailed

A mission statement is broad based and vision is detailed. Think about a vision that provides only the broad strokes, the general parameters within which you might operate. It does little to serve your ministry because it fails to provide direction. It does not allow you to filter opportunities and say no to those that would only dissipate your resources. It does not enable you to recruit people for meaningful outreach because the task seems too broad or because the purpose fails to motivate.

The danger exists, of course, of defining a vision so tightly that you become boxed in, limited as to what you can and cannot do. God's vision will not paint you into a corner. His vision frees you to do more than you might have conceived on your own but places valid and helpful parameters on where you are headed in pursuit of His glory.

Think about your reading of Scripture. How impressive it is that He is involved in and aware of even the most minor details of your life. And as you read the stories of the visionary leaders in the Bible, recognize how God has given them large-scale tasks with specific limitations and detailed guidance. He will do the same for you. Do not assume that you have grappled enough with the vision-capturing process if your understanding of His vision remains general and sketchy. Allow Him to fill in the details of the picture so that your efforts will achieve their optimal effect.

To define vision too tightly may box you in and limit what you can and cannot do.

Vision Is People Oriented

God is not a task-oriented ruler. He created people. He loves people. He sent His Son to die for the sins of people. He designed the church as a means for people to love others and to love Him. God is the ultimate people-Person.

In light of that, His vision for you will focus on how you can change the lives of people. Organizational development is useful. Buildings serve a purpose. Programs are a means to an end. But the end itself is always related to changing the lives of people.

Because of this, the vision takes into account the truth of human nature and the felt needs of people who must serve and be served in ministry. The vision also will reflect the highest value that can be achieved by man: a deeper relationship with God. As you examine your vision statement, ask whether it really centers on the importance of people's growth in faith and involvement with God. If the vision reflects any other bias, it is not from God. His vision for your ministry is the avenue through which you can facilitate personal spiritual growth among people.

Vision Reveals a Promising Future

Vision may awaken many other emotions within us, such as the following:

- Relief over having a viable purpose on Earth
- Joy over the realization that God can use us
- Confidence based on the notion that He will bless our faithfulness to His call

- Anticipation over the desire to see how the vision will look in practice and what impact it will have on people's lives
- Hope for the future, based on the recognition that He is in control and that we are truly on the winning side
- Passion to return to Him a measure of the love He has demonstrated by counting us worthy of His mercy, adequate to be part of His team and destined to see Him prevail
- Anxiety to get on with the tasks that will further promote righteousness, justice and love in a world that cries out for a better quality of life but has no clue as to where to search for it

Research consistently reveals that people in America want to make a difference in the world. For all their selfish tendencies and inward-looking practices, they want their lives to count for something of lasting value. The means to that end is loving and serving God. And the surest avenue to effectively growing that relationship is to capture His vision and live it to the fullest.

8

Your Ministry Will Benefit

Chapter Highlights

- Vision produces spiritual and emotional empowerment.
- Vision builds on the past.
- Vision elicits increased commitment from the congregation.
- Vision unifies God's people.

Chapter 8
Your Ministry Will Benefit

Jacques Plante, a goalie for a professional ice hockey team, had just come off the ice after a particularly poor performance and responded to a badgering reporter with the following remark: "How would you like a job where, if you made a mistake, a big red light goes on and 18,000 people boo?"

Pastors sometimes go through periods where they feel like they are in the same type of pressure cooker of responsibility and judgment. And while they may find some comfort that the pulpit does not have a flashing red light attached to signal a sloppy service or a poor sermon, they are aware of the same type of evaluation as the goalie experiences.

One of the greatest advantages of ministering in response to God's vision for your ministry is that much of the pressure is removed from your shoulders. Because you have been given a vision of a better future by the One who is perfect and seeks to make you successful in ministry, you can reach out with greater confidence and energy than might otherwise be possible.

Consider the following dozen benefits that you will enjoy as you minister in the strength of His vision for your future.

Big Dreams

How suffocating it can be to live within the boundaries of human ability. When we confine our thinking to the limitations of what is known, what we have experienced or what we are able to imagine, the mental playing field is relatively small.

When you have captured God's vision for your ministry, one of your first reactions will be, *But that's ridiculous; we could never do that.* If you persist, though, and conclude that this is what He is calling you to do, often you will recognize that His dreams are bigger than yours and that they call for you to expand the size of your mental playing field to accommodate His vision.

Great power can result from dreaming big. Such vision implies a long-term approach to ministry. Many leaders suffer from having constantly to rethink their vision because it was so small that they accomplished it quickly, or because it was so insignificant that it barely seemed worth the effort. God's vision for your life, though, is grand. His vision is not one you are likely to accomplish in a year or two. A few Christian visionaries have learned that once you catch His vision, it will outlive you. Your role is to grasp it, to articulate it and to ensure that it is acted upon. Your responsibility is not to see it come to a conclusion. Work toward that end, but do not feel incomplete if it is not fully accomplished in your lifetime. Simply being part of making that vision become a reality will seem like a sufficient reward.

Dreaming big, through God's enablement, is also one means of allowing the church to see and to reflect God's power and majesty. His desires are so much better and more meaningful than our own that when we envision them and fully support them, the spiritual and emotional empowerment is incredible. People become genuinely excited over the grand possibilities. The magnitude of the task is dwarfed by the realization that He wants to do it, and He intends to make it happen through you.

Continuity

One difficulty with the strategic ministry process at many churches is that it has a stutter effect. That is, lacking a long-term, significant vision ordained by God, the church jerks forward and then grinds to a halt each time it creates new goals and seeks to satisfy them. Little sense of accomplishment results because there are insufficient ties to a larger theme that runs through all of the ministry endeavors.

When you are working out God's vision, however, the journey will be smoother and more pleasing. His vision builds on the past rather than ignores it. His vision uses the fruit of past efforts rather than being paralyzed by the experience of the past. His vision materializes from what was learned and accomplished in an easy-flowing, natural manner.

Granted, we know that He is no respecter of persons. However, we also know that He respects the reality of your experience without being hindered by it. He uses that experience to build a reasonable future that best serves His purposes. He is never limited by your past but is always sensitive to it and creates a future that establishes a continuity for you.

BENEFIT 3

Direction and Purpose

You cannot be a true leader unless you are capable of charting a desired destination for your followers. God's vision allows you not only to identify the destination but also to articulate a clear reason for desiring that objective. A leader must have followers to be effective, and God's vision will enable you to present a clear view of where you are headed that will stir people to action.

You cannot be a true leader unless you are capable of charting a desired destination for your followers.

But followers are rarely mindless beings who pursue directives without questioning or a sense of wonder. Effective leaders are capable of explaining to people not simply the objective but also the reasons why that eventual outcome is desirable and how the group will arrive at that point. God's vision is deep enough to permit you to paint a mental portrait of the road of ministry and the destination for a congregation. Armed with that clarity, people are more likely to align their resources with that purpose in an efficient manner.

Increased Interest and Commitment

Churches often suffer from a lethargic laity. The people seem incapable of mustering any enthusiasm for ministry, resulting in efforts that lack energy and impact. I also have found that these churches are playing the church game without the benefit of God's vision at the core of their efforts.

One tremendous benefit of leaning on God's vision is that the church ceases to be a victim of circumstances. Pulsating with the belief that He has directed the ministry to pursue specific outcomes, the laity exhibit a renewed interest in and commitment to ministry. Believing that God is involved in their efforts, they become more aggressive at creating the desired future rather than waiting for that imagined scenario to happen. Instead of simply reacting to conditions, the people begin to formulate their own ministry environment by anticipating changes and fostering a world that enables them to be effective.

Acceptable Change

One outgrowth of real vision is change. Vision is the antithesis of the status quo. It mandates new approaches for new outcomes.

Most people, however, are uncomfortable with change. Thus, one of the most fundamental characteristics of vision (namely, change) causes people to be wary of the process and its products.

Thankfully, my observation is that when a leader ordained by God details His vision for His people, that discomfort level dissipates quickly. A residual of nagging fear and doubt about the ability to pull it off or the ultimate impact of their efforts may linger, but the uneasiness about pursuing the vision is largely eliminated. The fear of chaos and the anxiety of giving up what is known are replaced by a sense of peace that He is in control and has developed a better plan for His people.

Our distaste for change is usually emotional rather than intellectual.

Our distaste for change is usually emotional rather than intellectual. This is one way in which God's vision is clearly superior to that of humans. When people resist embracing a vision for the future that has been developed solely by man, there is little hope of reducing people's emotional anxieties through a continued exploration of the intellectual acceptability of the vision. When you are seeking to implement God's vision, however, He invariably brings a calmness and unity to His people that dissolves their fears and doubts. In the end, their faith in Him and His love for them win out over their innate worries about their personal inabilities.

Filter for Opportunities

In outlining the strategies and tactics inherent in putting the vision into action, controversy may arise; confrontation may occur; competition for control may ensue.

In situations in which a leader chosen by God has been entrusted with His vision, the church is provided with means of controlling events rather than being manipulated or controlled by them. Controversies become useful points of discussion to clarify the vision and to energize the people.

In fact, one of vision's greatest benefits is that it serves as a filter that allows people to say no to a variety of ministry opportunities. One of Satan's greatest weapons today is to breed confusion and dissension within the church by creating more needs in people and society than a given body of believers can possibly address. The natural tendency of a church is to try to be all things to all people, providing the insights and resources needed for people to handle any condition. The reality, however, is that a church cannot be effective in ministry if it spreads itself so thin that it does a mediocre job in a wide array of ministry opportunities.

The better strategy, the one that corresponds with godly, visionary leadership, is to do an excellent job in a limited number of ministry areas, allowing other groups within the body to use their unique gifts and vision to address those needs that are peripheral to your vision. It is the vision imparted by God that enables a leader to reject opportunities for ministry without suffering from guilt. Indeed, with Jesus as a role model (see Mark 1:36-39), we can take this approach with confidence and relief.

BENEFIT 7

Openness

A common complaint among the people attending a visionless church is that its ministry is predictable and routine. Interest in discussion and exploration of new territory are discouraged.

In a church pursuing God's vision, though, the opposite is true. A premium is placed upon new ideas. Not all of those ideas are warmly received or automatically embraced, of course, but the message to the people is that God wants to use them in ministry and their ideas count. New approaches, creative thoughts and interesting perspectives are not only acceptable but are esteemed as one means of keeping the vision fresh and alive.

Where God's vision is evident, you will notice that human idiosyncrasies abound. There is not a cookie-cutter approach to forming

Christians. Every Christian is not expected to possess the same look, the same character, the same interests and the same lifestyle. God has spelled out His principles for us in His Word, and they must serve as the guidelines within which we grow and take shape. But those guidelines provide enormous room for uniqueness and creativity. The church that restricts uniqueness prevents God from maximizing the gifts and differences He has instilled within His people.

In the vision-driven church, people rejoice in the freedom to be the people that God intended them to be, knowing that He intends to use them for His advantage, despite their faults, limitations and shortcomings.

Encouragement

We live in a world that increasingly reminds us of our limitations, which creates a sense of hopelessness and despair. Our families are dysfunctional. Our education is inadequate. Our relationships are based on selfishness. Our culture is founded on vacuous values. Our intellectual capacity is hindered by the use of less than 10 percent of our brain. Our physical abilities are impaired by the ingestion of harmful chemicals. The problems of the world are too big for one person to impact.

The church led by God's vision for outreach brims with confidence.

Apart from the negativity of the world, the church led by God's vision for outreach brims with confidence. It is a church that serves the Creator of the universe, the omnipotent Ruler of all things. It is a church that relishes rather than retreats from a stiff challenge because that confrontation simply provides the pedestal from which it can proclaim and demonstrate His power surging through them.

The church built on His vision knows it can make a difference in the world. Every individual within the congregation is meant to play a critical role in influencing the world for His glory in alignment with the corporate ministry vision. There is ample reason to be excited.

The church built on His vision is one that has higher expectations and therefore performs at a higher level. It is a community not content with simply getting by because that would result in outcomes that do not maximize the potential they have in God.

BENEFIT 9

Confidence

When people feel good about themselves, they perform better, they have greater endurance and they are less likely to burn out. In churches where God's vision is the heart of people's efforts, those characteristics are evident.

Because the people feel empowered by God, they rise to challenges they could not ordinarily dream of confronting. Their performance is generally above average because they recognize that they are pursuing a higher calling and have been granted the stamina and resources to accomplish that end.

Pride can contribute to a person's downfall. The Bible contains many stories of people whose leadership or daily lives were ruined by excessive pride in their own capabilities. In individuals who are part of a community seeking to serve God in conjunction with His vision, however, the pride that emanates from people is not a selfish pride but a selfless pride. They are excited to belong to the community of believers who have done a mighty work. They feel privileged to know and serve a God who loves them enough to give them an immense task to pursue and the resources to accomplish it. They are proud to be part of a world in which their lives make a difference.

BENEFIT 10

Loyalty

People no longer are loyal to products; instead, they buy the product that best meets their needs at the time of purchase (e.g., lowest price, most desirable quantity, most attractive packaging). People no longer are loyal to people. Look at the divorce rate, the loneliness of most Americans and the frequency with which people on the fast track in the business world use others for personal gain. Loyalty in the realm of religion is also uncommon as illustrated in the growth of church shopping and in the incidence of people embracing gods other than the Christian God.

An interesting consequence of vision is that people are more likely to feel they are truly part of the church.

What is missing for most people is a vision that focuses their loyalty. An interesting consequence of vision in vision-led churches is that people are more likely to feel that they are truly part of the church. They have a heightened sense of loyalty because they own the vision for ministry. This sharing of a common vision blends people together in a manner that otherwise may not be possible.

The vision shifts people's attention from failures to successes. Rather than pointing fingers of blame and worrying about damage control, vision-driven churches do not panic and disintegrate because they know they ultimately will be victorious. This faith in the future prepared by God causes them to view differences within the congregation not as weakness but as strength, not as divisive but as complementary.

Efficiency

When the vision is in place, a sense of urgency about ministry is present. Procrastination feels like sin. Because we never know how much time we have to transform our part of the world for God's glory, we cannot afford to assume that we can do ministry at a leisurely pace. Time is of the essence. The vision enables us not only to feel the urgency, but also to sustain the energy needed to accomplish the job efficiently.

I have yet to encounter a church that is so rich in resources that it can waste them in ministry and not feel pinched as a result. Because the world is so needy, we can expect to encounter a persistent demand for more tangible resources than we generally have available. Vision is one element that helps us to minimize the waste of our precious resources.

Often, people in leadership positions at churches attempt to discern vision through a process of trial and error. Eventually, perhaps by the process of elimination, the church will stumble upon a vision that seems workable. Unfortunately, along the way huge amounts of resources are consumed. People are burned out. Money is wasted. Time is lost. Credibility is tarnished. Gaining God's vision for your ministry by trial and error is the least effective and least efficient route to travel.

Productivity

When you have grasped His vision and are working toward it, you will likely find that a major benefit is a heightened level of productivity. With everyone seeking the same outcomes, with everyone working in harmony, the opportunities for a greater harvest are multiplied.

Vision allows those in ministry to create plans, strategies and tactics that result in better defined, highly targeted ministries. The result is more output per input.

In today's society, benefits are one of the keys to attracting employees, fans and even friends. You may not like living in a benefit-driven society because it smacks of selfishness. But it's the only society you've got.

Realistically, understanding the benefits of vision and describing those benefits for the people who must live the vision for effective ministry to occur is appropriate. Seeing the benefits of vision can be a powerful motivation for individuals to reprioritize their activities and resources. In this case, why not make a strong pitch in defense of the importance of pursuing vision even if it incorporates some emphasis upon personal benefits?

Vision Killers

Chapter Highlights

- One of the most popular and devastating barriers to true vision is the notion that God would never cause you to do something other than what you've always done before.
- Vision replaces fear with energy and hope.
- Christian culture and ministry are riddled with damaging stereotypes.
- Complacency is the extinguisher of the smoldering passion of vision.
- As a leader, you have the responsibility to overcome the inhibitors of God's vision.

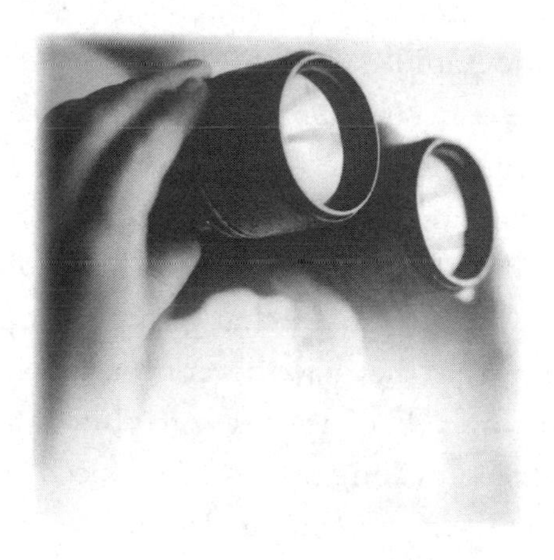

Chapter 9
Vision Killers

You will face stiff opposition from Satan as you seek to comprehend the vision that God has designed for your ministry. Your grasp of that vision will pound another nail in his coffin; he will do all he can to prevent you from absorbing God's vision.

Yet, probably the greatest obstacle you will face in the process may have little to do with Satan or demonic forces. Sometimes we give the devil more credit than he deserves. In many instances, rather than blame the devil, we should instead look in the mirror to find the real culprit.

Having examined the vision-capturing and vision-disseminating process in many churches, I have noticed a group of vision inhibitors that consistently emerge. These are beliefs, assumptions, practices and emotions that arise to prevent the vision from emerging or being widely accepted. By identifying these self-made barriers to vision, perhaps you can avoid falling prey to their debilitating effect on your ministry.

A pastor must think strategically if he wishes to counter vision killers. He must recognize the obstacles he will encounter and develop a strategy to overcome them.

Keep in mind, for example, that at least one segment of a congregation will say, "But we've never done it that way." One strategy would be to counter by showing how the church actually has accommodated change and how embarking upon change will give the church an edge in ministry. Be prepared to show that while no other church in the area has ever done it that way, the proposed change provides an opportunity to touch people in a way that they have never been touched.

Most leaders discover that they begin to think strategically as they work through the vision-making process. The focus of one new church, for example, was on seekers—unchurched people who have little interest in being in a church. With that in mind, the strategic factor came into play. When seekers visited the church, members knew these visitors were thinking, *What are you going to do for me?* Because seekers were part of the vision, members of the congregation needed to know how to respond by doing something that would impact the life of a non-Christian. When a church reaches this point, the pastor needs to teach the congregation how to build relationships with nonchurch people, what they are like, what they think about, what they do with their free time, what they think about the Bible, why they don't attend church. Then he might suggest how to meet these people and how to deal with them when they tell their four-letter-word jokes.

The pastor's challenge: How will I get Christians who have always been in churches that have targeted Christians to break habits developed over a lifetime? The response to that question is what makes the strategic perspective so important.

VISION KILLER

Tradition

One of the most popular and devastating barriers to true vision is the notion that God would never cause you to change what you have always done before. This usually is expressed through such exclamations as "But we've never done it that way before."

In reality, God uses traditions in ministry to provide people with a semblance of consistency and stability. Traditions can form a foundation upon which He builds the future. Traditions can serve as a bridge between the past and the future, enabling people to retain a comfort zone while focusing on Him.

But God has no use for traditions that block progress. He blesses those traditions that build the church and His people, not because they are traditions but because they serve His purposes. Indeed, He tends to reshape traditions by moving them in new directions. He updates them with a more relevant and contemporary expression of those truths that made the tradition valuable initially. But His primary concern is not with the style or format of the tradition; His interest is in its ability to draw people closer to Him.

Tradition is generally a reflection of the past. Vision is always a reflection of the future. Is there any room for a marriage between the two? Absolutely! Because He is the God who created and reigned over the past, He can use history to His advantage in your life and ministry. He has no reason to blot out all memory of the past or to deny its value and power. Instead, it is likely that He will continue to move you in a ministry direction that helps you mature. Maturity means growing beyond your past and embodies what and where you have been. He will use your past to enhance your future.

In your ministry, acknowledge your past for what it has been. Recognize the traditions and patterns that enabled you to impact people's lives for His glory. Use those as stepping-stones, building your ministry for maximum impact. Determine how you can honor your past by incorporating past strengths into your future.

VISION KILLER

Fear

Grasping and implementing God's vision can be a frightening prospect. As mentioned earlier, vision requires change. Change means breaking out of the comfort zone, doing new things or operating in areas in which we lack a track record of success or substantial levels of self-confidence. Change can be scary. Moving in new directions or attempting new methods of ministry is risky. Risk raises the possibility of failure, and none of us want to fail, especially in ministry.

Sometimes we are overcome by fear because we have failed in the past and dare not reach for the stars again. Sometimes we dwell on our past failures or our sense of limitation. Rather than define defeat as either repeating the same mistake or refusing to take a risk, we think of it as not reaching our goals. We then allow the fear of failure to restrict our universe of opportunities to those that are safe. By focusing on our failings, we miss out on our potential.

We also experience fear in situations that we cannot control completely. Few Christians, leaders or not, arrive at a point where they totally release the reins of their lives and allow God to rule every moment of every day. We often lack faith the size of a mustard seed. In its place, we assert our authority over our destiny. Consequently, we are paralyzed by fear, limited in our ability to forge new trails for God's glory.

Sometimes we are overcome by fear because we have failed in the past and dare not reach for the stars again.

Vision replaces fear with energy and hope. It dismisses unbelief and replaces it with peace and assurance. Vision raises questions, but it does not raise nagging doubts.

If you are beset by fear about the future or fear about the vision He has entrusted to you, recognize that fear for what it is: lack of faith in God's ability to work through you for His purposes. Pray through the fear. Abdicate control of your ministry to Him. Believe that He can do what He desires to do.

VISION KILLER

Stereotypes

A stereotype is a popular preconception about people or conditions. American culture is saturated with stereotypes. Christian culture and ministry, too, are riddled with them.

Recently I encountered dozens of stereotypes in churches, all of which I tested and found to be untrue. A church in Arizona persisted with traditional organ music on Sundays because its membership was elderly. It was discovered, however, that members were sick of that style of music and desired something a bit more modern and lively. A pastor in Alabama confided that his church was in turmoil over the role of women and how centuries-old stereotypes about their abilities and gifts prevented them from serving in biblical ways. Stereotypes regarding racial and ethnic characteristics, versions of the Bible, styles of preaching, the educational capacity of certain schools, the acceptability of styles of music and many other elements have caused divisiveness and hardship within the Church and have prevented us from penetrating the world beyond the sanctuary walls.

Stereotypes are sometimes used as shortcuts to truth. However, such shortcuts do not exist. In contrast, God's vision for your ministry is founded on truth. It requires that you see yourself and the world realistically and respond in a realistic manner. Following stereotypes leads to bad decisions. Following God's vision leads to wise decisions if you have cleansed your mind and heart of the erroneous perceptions that may be reflected in stereotypes.

VISION KILLER

Complacency

Sometimes we fail to behave with vigor and passion because we are ignorant or complacent: "It doesn't matter what we do; God will bless our efforts." This statement is a prescription for half-baked, half-blessed ministry. He does care what we do. If He didn't care, He would not have given dreams and words to the prophets. In fact, He would not have provided prophets. If He didn't care, He would not ask us to seek His guidance and ask for His blessing. If He didn't care, He would not have allowed certain passages of the Bible to become part of the canon (e.g., Luke 14:28-32; Jas. 2:14-17; Rev. 3:15-18).

God's passion for mankind is evident in the story of Jesus Christ. The passion of visionary leaders like Paul and David is evident in their works. Complacency is the extinguisher of that smoldering passion.

Once the passion has been extinguished, we are of little value in the raging fight between the powers of light and darkness. Those who reflect complacency and ignorance will be the next casualties on the spiritual battlefield.

As you evaluate your quest for His vision, test your passion quotient. Are you ready to give it all you've got? Would you die for the chance to see that vision become reality? Do you care enough about your relationship with Him and for the deployment of the vision He gives you to put everything you have on the line? Is your church so lethargic that the prospects of fulfilling the vision are slim? If you are serious about serving Him to the fullest, identify those people whose hearts are lukewarm and avoid letting them hinder the process.

VISION KILLER

Fatigue

Ministry is not easy. Even the greatest spiritual warriors need times of rest. Jesus took time for solitude. If you have difficulty generating excitement about the vision or if you have trouble grasping the vision, check to see if you are running on empty. Vision calls for a tremendous degree

As a leader grappling with matters of universal and eternal significance, you must be rested before beginning the journey.

of faith and energy. Seeking vision when you are exhausted makes no sense. Your natural inclination will be to resist those perspectives that call for you to break down known barriers and to redefine the known. Fatigue will limit your vision and your influence for Him.

I also have witnessed cases in which a congregation has essentially rejected God's vision because it, as an entity, was too spent from recent battles and victories to entertain the prospect of climbing new spiritual mountains. It is the wise leader who prepares the church body to hear and to embrace that vision by persuading them to rest for the next leg of the journey.

As a leader grappling with a matter of universal and eternal significance, you, too, must be well rested before embarking on the vision-seeking journey. Prepare for the challenge by recharging your mental, emotional and spiritual batteries. When you are energized for the challenge, move forward.

VISION KILLER

Short-Term Thinking

Today, leaders are increasingly interested in cashing in resources for short-term benefits. The tragedy is that it leaves nothing in place for the long run. To follow such a course robs us of a satisfying future by chasing immediate gratification. We deplete the past to enjoy the present at the expense of the future.

The truth is, however, that God's vision for ministry is long-term in nature. His vision may well outlive the visionary. His goals are eternal, not temporal. His knowledge and resources are unlimited, enabling us to pursue a vision for which He will be responsible to the end.

His timing is often different from our own. He is not pressured by time. He has created a season for each good thing and knows the appropriate pace for life. His timing is perfect. We should pursue the vision in concert with His timing. Rather than seek quick results and tangible benefits in the short term, how much better it would be to dream the big dream and to be part of the fundamental transformation of people's lives and of entire cultures. His vision may lead you to such grandiose activities. Define your measures of success in ministry so that you respond to His timing, not the world's timing.

In the end, you are the only person who can limit your ability to dream big with God. As a leader, you have a responsibility to recognize and overcome the inhibitors of God's vision. If you are truly committed to capturing His vision for your ministry, then see the pitfalls for what they are: danger zones to be avoided. They are not obstacles that should remove you from the action on the spiritual playing field.

Articulating the Vision

Chapter Highlights

- Growth is more likely to occur in churches where there is clear, substantive, productive communication taking place on a regular basis.
- Vision must be owned.
- Vision must be spelled out for everyone associated with it.
- Vision statements are critical; they must be focused and concise.

Chapter 10

Articulating the Vision

Over the past decade, I have had an opportunity to work with some of the leading corporations in the country, studying their plans, strategies and methods of implementation. Certain patterns have emerged that relate to the ability of those corporations to meet their goals.

One of the most consistent of those patterns relates to the ability to communicate effectively. Simply put, the organizations that have efficient, clear, reliable means of communication tend to be successful; those whose lines of communication are underdeveloped, imprecise or otherwise restricted are more likely to experience stagnation or decline.

Churches are no different. In those churches where clear, substantive, productive communication takes place consistently, growth is more likely to occur than in churches where effective communication is a hit-or-miss affair.

Articulating the vision is one of the most important types of communication. Having a true vision is of little value unless it can be communicated with clarity and consistency.

As you work through the vision-making process, realize that once you have captured God's vision for your ministry, you must develop it for two audiences: yourself and those people with whom you will be ministering. While the vision itself will remain the same, the depth and manner with which you describe it will be different in each of those cases.

Understand the Vision

There is no chicken-egg dilemma here. Clearly, you must understand the vision in all its scope and nuances before you can hope to describe all of its dimensions to other people. You are the initial audience for God's vision for your ministry. He is entrusting it to you.

When I was young, I played football. Generally I was an end, meaning that my primary task was to run downfield and elude defenders so I could catch a pass from our quarterback. In studying the moves and abilities of professional pass receivers, I noticed one important quality: A well-thrown pass often was dropped because the receiver took his eye off the ball before he caught it. In his haste to gain as much ground as possible, the receiver began running before he had full ownership of the pigskin.

Vision Must Be Owned

Vision is the same way. You must take time to understand the full dimensions of the vision before you can live it yourself and motivate others to embrace it and to run with it.

Your personal goal ought to be to clarify the vision in all its details, to plant it so completely in your mind and heart that it becomes part of who you are and to train yourself to use it as your filter for responding to all situations you encounter.

One potential conflict to be resolved concerns distinguishing the vision for your personal ministry from the vision for corporate ministry. I have encountered pastors and other church leaders who were certain they had captured God's vision for the ministry of the congregation but felt the vision for their personal ministry did not parallel that of the church. Thus, while they consistently modeled the vision in their ministry activities, as teacher or leader or shepherd of the flock, they also felt they were called to specific avenues of personal ministry that were somewhat different from the direction in which the church was headed.

For instance, one pastor was leading a church whose ministry was to reach Baby Boomers who had left the church. The congregation swelled every month with new adults in their 30s and 40s who found the music, teaching and social networking appealing and uplifting. On Saturday mornings, however, the pastor did not play softball with fellow Boomers. He spent Saturday mornings ministering to people at a nursing home in a neighboring town. He was at a loss to explain the apparent contradiction in his focus. His best explanation was that perhaps God wanted him to be sensitive to all types of people and thus moved him to build bridges with older adults, even in the midst of building an exploding ministry to young adults.

Your personal vision probably incorporates a core aspect of the church's vision plus some areas designed to set you apart.

Realize that God's vision for you, personally, probably incorporates a core aspect of the church's vision plus a few peripheral areas that are designed solely for you apart from the efforts of the church. You are not the entire church; you are part of the church. You are called to invest your best efforts in its work. But you are also part of the larger Body of Christ, the Church. As such, you have responsibilities to use your gifts and opportunities to reflect His love, grace and power, perhaps in ways that are unrelated to the central workings of your congregation.

Put the Vision on Paper

You will profit by writing the vision for the church's ministry in as comprehensive a fashion as possible. Perhaps that comprehensive statement will never be seen by anyone but you. By documenting your thoughts in detail, you can return to the statement periodically to review whether you are on course, to determine if dimensions or nuances of the vision have been overlooked, to remind yourself of the power and depth of the vision and to become reinvigorated by that reintroduction to His dream for your work.

Return to your comprehensive vision statement during those times when you are involved in planning the future work of the congregation. Vision is useful only if it is implemented; implementation occurs most effectively when matters are planned and strategies for application are thought through and are meticulously carried out. Vision is the centerpiece of strategy; strategy is the means to effective church development; effective development of the church is the means to transforming the world with His love. Be sure that when strategic decisions and plans are being conceived, the vision is the heart of the discussion. As God's appointed leader, you are the protector of that vision and must be responsible for seeing that all strategic and tactical decisions accurately reflect the vision.

Help the Church Understand the Vision

When your understanding of the vision is in place, your colleagues at the church must also grasp the picture. Just as Moses was entrusted with disseminating the information on the stone tablets, so you are responsible for helping people understand and absorb the insights that are part of the vision for the church.

In articulating the vision for people, recognize that it must be presented within a meaningful context.

In articulating the vision for the people, recognize that it must be presented within a meaningful context. Vision must be viewed as a direction provided by God and as a strategic framework for ministry. It is not simply a statement of nice ideas that might work if we are blessed. It is a directive that we must obey, praying for His blessing and utilizing all of the energy and resources at our disposal. His vision is His set of marching orders for us to follow.

Spell It Out for Everyone

Toward that end, develop a public reference document that outlines the key elements of the vision for the church's ministry. This document will differ from the document you have prepared for yourself. The difference is analogous to the script received by an actor and that possessed by the director of a film. The actor's script contains the vital information he needs: the lines, key movements, specific places to be. The director's script, however, contains more detail: camera angles, lighting notations and staging reminders. The heart of the content is the same, but the elements on the perimeter differ according to the needs and role of the reader.

When the vision is articulated for people, make certain they understand that God's vision is not simply a series of deeds that happen in a corporate setting. The vision for church is meant to be lived at all times of the day and night by people in whatever circumstances they find themselves. Help your people understand the broad implications of the vision for their lives by explaining how they might capture the totality of the vision and take it to the streets.

Keep It Short

Don't fool yourself. People do not remember reams of information. Give them a 10-page report to read and they will retain a few facts that strike them as central to the thesis or as intriguing anomalies. Give them a book and they will recall relatively little beyond some of the mental imagery it conveys and a handful of key points. People's recall of information is less extensive than we would like.

As Robert Greenleaf once said, "Many attempts to communicate are nullified by saying too much." The words of advertising executive Al Ries confirm the thought: "We have become the world's first overcommunicated society. Each year we send more information and receive less."

One Paragraph Will Suffice

Given this reality, do not try to articulate the vision in a lengthy written format. Most people will not read it. Those who do will forget most of what they read within a few hours. The KISS principle (keep it short and simple) works very well when articulating the vision. You can give people the bigger picture, complete with details. In fact, it is important to do so to communicate the larger context. However, when providing people with a document that they will use as their focus for the vision, limit it to one short paragraph.

Many leaders resist this reductionistic practice and argue that God's vision cannot be limited to two or three sentences.

Many leaders resist this reductionistic practice, arguing that God's vision cannot be limited to two or three sentences. My experience has been that convincing the church to embrace any communiqué that is more extensive leads to problems. More important, I have found that leaders who cannot capture the essence of the vision within three sentences probably have not clarified it in their own minds to make it a workable vision.

Get Down to Basics

When you reduce the vision to a few sentences, you have stripped away all but the heart of the matter. And that is precisely what people need to keep in front of them, not the nuances, not the outer limits, not the ramifications, but the core of the dream God has provided to the church. For the vision to be effective—i.e., to act as a filter, to stimulate enthusiasm, to motivate involvement, to understand the focus of the ministry, to promote widespread ownership of the vision—it must be simple enough to be remembered and specific enough to give direction. Ownership is a necessity. People must feel they can customize the vision within the boundaries of the church's unique personality and outreach and can add to it through their own comprehension and application.

Here are some critical elements to incorporate into your vision statement. Identify what type of people you are called to minister to: a specific age group, a personality type, a lifestyle segment, a geographic area. Clarify the purpose of your efforts to reach those people: to introduce them to Christ in a nonthreatening way, to bring unchurched Christians back into the church, to disciple believers, to build a core of socially conscious believers who will address current issues and so forth. (Remember, your goal is to focus, so do not simply repeat the ministry objectives identified in your mission statement.) Indicate the qualities that make your church distinctive from others in the area: the target audience, the ministry format or some other point of differentiation.

Generally, I have found that churches do best when they capture these key points in no more than five or six crucial thoughts.

Create the Vision Statement

How do you create a vision statement that is short, simple and memorable and yet effectively directs the path of the ministry? Here are some principles learned from studying how other churches have done it.

Acceptable Concepts

Design a statement that makes sense to everyone: non-Christians, new Christians, mature Christians, inert Christians, active believers and church staff. Because vision defines the church's efforts, it must be a statement that is shared with those who are exploring a longer-term relationship with the congregation. Because it must be motivating, it should be a statement that appeals to all of the people whom God truly desires to be part of that congregation. Because it must lead to excitement and to better decision making, it must focus on the positive while tacitly indicating the boundaries beyond which the church will not move.

Vivid Language

Because vision concerns a preferable future, that future takes shape in people's minds when an attractive mental picture of the future is painted. Use words that are active, compelling and appealing. The tone should be upbeat. The task must seem reasonable. Inspire people through the responsibilities, challenges and approaches alluded to in the statement.

Little is gained by using terms that people must struggle to understand. Theological terms and those that require some type of specialized training or knowledge undermine the clarity of statement. Keep the words short, the thoughts crisp, the outcomes evident. Because you are limited to just two or three sentences, do not attempt to stretch the limits by writing sentences that would ordinarily be a paragraph long.

Shelve the Slogans

You probably have run across many churches that believe they have captured their vision through the use of a catchy slogan.

- To win the lost at any cost
- Reach 2,010 by 2010
- Share if you care, then sow to grow
- A church that will worship, reach, build and pray
- Evangelize, edify and empower
- Training workers to reap the harvest

One problem with most slogans that purportedly communicate the vision is that they do not communicate vision. Most slogans simply reflect the mission of the church.

Simplicity, Not Triviality

Another serious problem is that the slogans frequently trivialize rather than simplify the vision. It is easy to lose sight of the significance of the

One problem with most slogans is that they reflect the mission rather than the vision of a church.

cause when a few snappy words have been strung together. Trivial slogans are memorable, yes. But effective? No.

Using a slogan or theme line to promote the vision is a perfectly acceptable approach as long as the vision is not undermined in the process. Advertisers pay agencies thousands of dollars to develop memorable tag lines, not because they want to spread their profits around, but because creating a workable, influential, substantive line is not a simple procedure. As many advertisers have learned the hard way, leaning on a weak line can harm the product. Similarly, a church can be hurt by reducing its most important statement about future ministry to a saccharine, relatively generic grouping of words.

THE TRICKLE-DOWN EFFECT

CHAPTER HIGHLIGHTS

- To be effective, the vision must be shared and omnipresent.
- Expose people to the vision through your sermon topics and content, through all written communication and in all group contexts.
- Employ a variety of people to help cast the vision.
- Vision is disseminated through the trickle-down process.

Chapter 11

The Trickle-Down Effect

My introduction to research and marketing was in the political arena. After serving for several years as a campaign manager for individuals seeking election to public office, I returned to graduate school to study political affairs in more detail. During that period, I was intrigued by the widespread enjoyment of critiquing the president. Everyone seemed to have an opinion about how well the president was doing his job. Studying those opinions, as we have done in some of our research, can lead to some humorous, frightening and comforting realizations, depending on whose opinions are being examined.

How frustrating to find a church that is anxious to follow its leader but has no idea in what direction it is being led.

Jimmy Carter as a president was particularly fascinating. He was generally viewed as a good person but as an ineffective leader. I believe part of his difficulty in the Oval Office was that he had a vision for America that was never clearly articulated. Although the oddsmakers in Las Vegas initially said he was a 1,000-to-1 long shot, he was motivated to run for the presidency by the vision he had for the nation. Unfortunately, that vision was never developed, explained and nurtured in such a way that it became widely shared by his colleagues in government and by the people he was elected to lead. The vision never extended much beyond 1600 Pennsylvania Avenue.

How frustrating to find a church that is anxious to follow its leader but has no idea in what direction it is being led. It is especially discouraging to visit a church where the leader has God's vision for the church's ministry but has simply overlooked a crucial step in the process: disseminating the vision so that it can be owned and implemented by the congregation.

Give It Away

The vision is meant to be shared. That can only happen when it is clear and when it is available. But how does a church leader make that vision available and accessible to the people in the church?

One of the most important decisions a leader makes is how to cast the vision. Those leaders who have been most successful contend that you must take advantage of all opportunities, at all times, to share the vision.

The communication process should begin, however, at the beginning. Don't surprise the congregation by announcing, "I have been concerned for some time that we've been a visionless congregation and have prepared a vision statement for us to follow."

As you begin seeking God's direction in creating a vision statement, let your congregation know that you are wrestling with God on the question of what He really wants of the congregation. Hopefully, this will build a sense of excitement within the congregation much like this: "We're getting in tune with God. When the pastor has grasped that clarified vision, we're going to have our work cut out for us. We're going to make a great impact on our community."

Strategically, it is helpful to let the congregation know in the beginning that a process is under way. As the pastor, invite the support of your congregational members, ask for their thoughts and for their prayers. Create a sense of togetherness, a sense that you and they are God's team here. You are elected captain of the team, but you can't do it without their help.

Several avenues for communicating the vision may be available to you in your church.

Sermons

The content of your sermons, for example, should reflect the substance of your vision. The teaching should enable people to understand how the vision can become ingrained in their thoughts and activities and to see how vision was modeled on the lives of biblical characters. Keep in mind that some visionary pastors evaluate the utility of a sermon topic

Teaching should enable people to understand how the vision can be ingrained in their thoughts and activities.

according to whether it fits within the vision for ministry of the church and how adequately they can tie that subject to the vision.

Printed Materials

Most churches have a bulletin or printed program that is handed out at services as well as a weekly or monthly newsletter. Those are ideal opportunities to display the vision so that people have constant, tangible exposure to the content. Other printed materials, such as the annual report or the visitor's welcome packet, should incorporate that statement.

Letters

Pastors often send letters to the congregation. What a wonderful opportunity to call people's attention to the vision. Also, consider including the vision statement as part of the church's letterhead.

Teaching

Visionary leaders encourage everyone who teaches on behalf of the church—in Sunday School classes, small-group studies, leadership retreats—to incorporate an understanding and statement of the vision into their teaching. Do not neglect the new-member class, either. What better time to introduce the vision and its implications for lifestyle and ministry than when an individual is evaluating a church or making a commitment to that body?

Meetings

Many churches include prayer in all of their meetings. Why not include some mention of the vision in the proceedings as well? Effective churches generally find that their decision-making process is more efficient and effective when the vision is used as a filter through which important decisions are made.

Multiple Vision Casters

The efforts of effective church-based visionaries also demonstrate the imperative of having multiple vision casters. The point person in the ministry is generally the senior pastor. He or she must consistently communicate and staunchly defend that vision. But if the pastor is the only individual who is promoting the vision, the church will not become a vision-driven entity.

The presence of multiple vision casters indicates that the vision is shared by a variety of people. Much as advertising theory teaches that the message is more likely to penetrate a potential customer's mind through repeated exposure, so must the faithful have multiple interactions with the vision. Having those interactions occur as a result of exposure to the vision from various people is advantageous.

Implementing the Vision

Keep in mind that vision operates on a trickle-down process. Initially the leader grasps the vision. He or she then shares it with the church staff. When they understand and embrace it, they articulate it for the lay leaders. They, in turn, will share the vision with the rest of their contacts in the church. At this stage, the vision has trickled down through the entire structure of the body. In fact, by the time the vision has been cast among the congregation at large, they are likely to hear the vision being articulated in many forms by many people who have decided to own it as their call in corporate ministry.

The Strategic Perspective

The application of the vision in all church-based endeavors ought to begin with the strategic perspectives of the church. Vision is critical for effective strategic planning and implementation. The ministry tactics utilized by the church should fully reflect the vision. In the process of marketing the church and its ministries, vision must be present. It is around the vision that all plans are made. Individuals who seek to bring marketing techniques to the ministry without a sensitivity to the realities of the vision do the church a great disservice.

When a strategic plan has been adopted, the role of the vision shifts to that of serving as a filter for key decisions. By examining all decisions and opportunities in light of the vision, the church can ensure that quality and direction in all ministry efforts is consistent with that called for by the vision. Often, churches base critical decisions on emotion, expediency or available resources. When vision is the centerpiece of the decision-making and evaluation processes, such ill-advised efforts are less likely to occur.

A Built-In Standard

In fact, the vision is also disseminated more deeply when it is not simply a statement of a desired outcome but is integrated into the ministry as a standard to be met. For instance, one means of integration would be to use it as the basis for measuring or evaluating the success of programs. Instead of using numbers or maintenance as the yardstick of success, the vision would likely provide the evaluators with different criteria for assessing an outreach effort. By constantly referring to the strategic goals and their basis, people become accustomed to thinking about the evaluative role vision plays in their ministry efforts.

Because every church has a unique approach to creating its programs and involving its people, numerous ways are available to layer the vision into the ministry process. The undisputed fact remains, however, that the ministry's effectiveness is enhanced when the vision is clear, shared and integrated into the efforts of everyone involved in the church's ministry.

12

Count the Cost

Chapter Highlights

- Capturing the vision can be a lonely and exhausting process.
- God's vision for your ministry may require you to learn new skills or to create new systems within your church.
- You may realize that you are being called to a different ministry.
- Expect Satan to confront you as you strive to gain God's vision.

Chapter 12

Count the Cost

The expression "anything good is worth paying for" is certainly true of God's vision for your ministry. And make no mistake about it, you will pay a price for your commitment to the vision.

The most immediate price you will pay is that of lost supporters. Because vision means change, some people will resist the prospect of change until it becomes evident they are fighting a losing battle. Merely dealing with resistance to the vision will be tough. But handling the departures from the body caused by the articulation of the vision will be even tougher. Some of your people will fight the vision but ultimately will surrender and play by the new rules. Others may leave the church for a more comfortable church setting. Vision stirs the dust that may have settled. Be willing to endure the trauma or leave the leadership duties to someone who is willing to do so. Realize that the people who cannot accept the vision God has for the church are simply in the wrong church at that time. To keep them in the congregation for selfish reasons would be to no one's advantage.

It's a Lonely Vigil

Capturing the vision and making it come alive for people can also be an excruciatingly lonely process for some leaders.

First, the vision-capturing process may be an ordeal. Hours and hours will be spent in prayer, in study, in counseling with others and in reviewing market information. Some leaders find this period very lonely; others find it to be exhilarating.

Second, the process of articulating the vision to the staff and to the congregation may be difficult. Sometimes this, too, can be a time of relative isolation as people distance themselves from you until they feel comfortable with the new—perhaps the radically new—direction you are promoting. Finally, the use of the vision as the mediator of all decisions, plans and evaluations can cause you to be seen in a new, and not always positive, light.

Capturing the vision and making it come alive for people can be an excruciatingly lonely process for some leaders.

You will pay a price in terms of energy expended to establish the vision. People must be educated. Influencers must be influenced. Key workers must be retrained. New modes of communication must be developed. Ministries and programs must be redesigned to match the vision. Strained relationships must be healed and strengthened.

In fact, you may have to learn new skills: vision casting, strategic planning based on vision, evaluations based on vision. This is a time to be stretched.

During the process, you may gain personal insights that are not easy to accept. Those often relate primarily to the areas in which you lack skills or gifts. Sometimes they relate to personal failures that are brought to the surface by the self-discovery process that precedes the clarification of the vision. Perhaps you may realize that God wants you in a different place for a different type of ministry at this time. None of these is easy to accept.

Some Won't Welcome Change

Be forewarned that promoting the vision will create discomfort for some people in your church. Some will agitate, constantly raising irritating questions about the necessity for change. Others will become so distraught that they will leave the congregation. Do not fret over such departures. Everyone grows differently. As the church moves in one direction, God may be calling those people to grow in a different way. That may mean introducing them to a different body, one that is more aligned with their views. Vision sometimes has a cleansing element to it, which reflects changing needs, conditions and growth. These changes can be emotionally painful, but they can be healthy for the church.

You Get to Forge Ahead

When it comes to maturing as a Christian, we know that we will encounter resistance from Satan. Growing in our faith is never an easy task, nor a painless one. The Bible even promises us some tough times in the process (see 2 Cor. 12:7-10).

When it comes to maturing as a Christian, we know that we will encounter resistance from Satan.

But just as the Bible promises tough times, it also promises that God will be present when we need extra strength and motivation. He will provide for our needs as we seek to serve Him. The same will be true for you as you pursue His vision and endeavor to implement it with fervor and passion for His glory. Count on tough times. But know that He will not forget you in those moments of doubt and difficulty.

Like many who have sought a vision that will build His kingdom for His glory, you might question why you are worrying about His vision when your intention has been to serve Him. The real question is how you could possibly engage in meaningful and effective ministry without allowing Him to be truly at the center of that effort.

Be encouraged that none of the visionaries I have met whose lives were dedicated to serving God with all their might has indicated that ministering from the basis of the vision was a wasted effort. None of those individuals said he or she would consider doing anything else, having experienced the joy of being so fully aligned with His purpose.

13

Capturing a Personal Vision

Chapter Highlights

- You, too, should develop a personal vision statement.
- The process requires study, prayer and thought.
- You may need special counseling.
- The results may be life changing.

CHAPTER 13

CAPTURING A PERSONAL VISION

The focus of this book so far has been on the vision God imparts to the pastor for his church's ministry. But every Christian is expected to live each waking moment in light of the special calling God has placed on his life. That special ministry He has designed for you is His vision for your personal ministry.

A pastor has been given a special privilege and a responsibility in leading a church. God entrusts His vision to the pastor to guide him in leading the congregation in its ministry and overall development.

In the same way, God expects each of us, whether we lead a church or not, to take command over our lives and use them to further His kingdom. Every Christian is called to live a life of ministry. Our greatest obligation while we are on Earth is to know God more intimately and to bring ever greater glory to His name by our efforts. To assist us in that effort, God wants to share with you His vision for your life and ministry.

THE PROCESS

Just as the pastor is the leader of a church, you are called to be the leader of your personal ministry and to live that ministry in accordance with God's expectations and desires for you, as outlined through the vision.

In much the same way that a pastor pursues the identity of God's vision for the ministry of the church, so should you, as an individual believer, seek to determine what is God's vision for your life and ministry. The process described earlier in this book—knowing yourself, knowing your circumstances, knowing God and receiving the discerning counsel of others—is the same procedure you ought to follow in capturing His vision for your life. Follow the same steps to understand what God has set aside for you as the special task He wants you to accomplish.

As an individual believer seeking the vision, each of us balances the input that leads us to a conclusion in a different way. Chances are good, for example, that you might spend more time seeking the advice of your pastor, treating him as your chief counselor in this process. Similarly, in knowing yourself, you may wish to avail yourself of different types of tests (such as the Meyers-Briggs personality test or a spiritual gifts test) to gain new insights into how God has built you. The ways you use information about the ministry environment may also differ from the manner the church pursues it.

Keys in the process, however, remain: prayer; studying His Word; seeking objective assessments of what you are experiencing in direction; and maintaining a diligent, patient, aggressive pursuit of the vision. It generally takes pastors a significant period of time to understand clearly the vision for the church. So, too, will you have to commit yourself to persevere until the vision for your own ministry is clear in your heart.

Aggressively seek to understand what God is calling you to do that distinguishes you from every other believer and that makes you a unique ambassador for Christ.

How sad it is that most Christians in America do not have a worldview or a philosophy of life that influences their decisions and lifestyles. Even fewer have worked through the process of gaining God's special gift of insight for their lives. Don't be among those who have overlooked this critical dimension of the Christian life. Like Paul, Nehemiah, David and other great people of faith, aggressively seek to understand what He is calling you to do that distinguishes you from every other believer and that makes you a unique ambassador for Christ.

Minister in Your Church, in Concert with Your Vision

Ultimately, your ministry will become more tangible and bear greater fruit as you live your life in a manner that is dedicated to making the vision a reality. Your personal sense of ministry impact and personal worth will soar as you move closer to fulfilling the vision.

Once you have ascertained the vision God has for your personal ministry, part of the challenge before you is to determine how to fulfill that calling within the context of the vision He has provided for your church. Each of us is called to be an integral part of the body of believers. At the same time, we are also expected to use our particular gifts and talents to satisfy the vision for our lives. Take time to determine how you can blend these two avenues of ministry into a consistent outreach effort. You will find that the church is most successful when the people that comprise the body have worked out ways of incorporating their unique skills and calling within the parameters of the church's corporate vision. This takes time to understand and to work out. Invest yourself in that process.

His Vision Reflects the Real You

As you seek God's vision for your life, remember that it will be a reflection of your unique characteristics and the yearnings He has placed within you. Your personality, your past experiences and your context for ministry will converge to result in a ministry that is uniquely you and that is important in the overall growth of God's work on Earth.

The heart of God's vision for your life's ministry will be serving people. If you feel drawn to an organizational vision or a structural vision, spend more time in prayer, counsel and study to understand how such a ministry can ultimately make a difference in the lives of people. God is not so much interested in organization or administration—although those skills are necessary in ministry—as in changing people's lives. When we serve people, we serve God; and His deepest desire is that we love Him by loving His people. View your vision in light of how your life will be geared to loving people and meeting their needs.

Facilitate Accountability in Your Ministry

Chances are good that nobody will challenge you regarding your vision—unless you ask a trusted, close ministry peer to hold you accountable. Although churches, as organizations, are likely to be challenged about their vision, most Christians do not have the privilege of being in a relationship in which they are held accountable. Set yourself up for success in ministry by arranging with one or more trusted colleagues in ministry to check in with you regularly to determine if you are really pouring your energies into pursuing the vision. Take their admonitions seriously, knowing that God places such comrades in your midst as a checkpoint.

Let your vision move you into areas of outreach that may be uncomfortable but will contribute to your personal growth.

In pursuing the vision, prepare to be stretched and challenged beyond your comfort zone. God's vision for your ministry, like the one He prepares for a church, will cause you to grow by demanding that you change, sharpen your skills and participate in situations in which your only hope of success is enabling His Spirit to guide you and empower you. Without the drive of the vision, chances are good that you would avoid these situations. Let the vision move you into areas of outreach that may be uncomfortable but will contribute to your personal growth. Let Him stretch you and thereby help you become a more capable minister for His kingdom.

Articulating the Vision

To increase the chances of truly pursuing the vision, articulate it for yourself in the same way a church must articulate the corporate vision for its people—in simple language, in a brief statement. Develop a one- or two-sentence statement regarding your vision, and constantly remind yourself that this is God's desire for you. Pray daily for Him to bless the vision and your efforts to fulfill it. Use your vision as the decision-making filter that determines which opportunities you pursue and which ones you reject. Use the vision as your moral and ethical compass when examining the broad range of behaviors you could pursue in the course of your daily activities.

As you strengthen and focus your ministry, with the help of your vision, other believers will be attracted to you and desire to discover what makes you so effective in ministry. Be prepared to help them understand the value of vision and what it has meant in your ministry. Even if you do not see yourself as a leader, when you devote yourself to implementing God's vision, you will have opportunities to help others in their personal spiritual growth by leading them in the vision-development process. This, in itself, represents another ministry in which you can help people.

Appendix 1

Bible Studies on Vision

The following Bible studies can be used to help you share the principles of godly vision and marketing with your church leadership team or congregation.

These studies are meant to be a tangible step for beginning the vision-casting process as articulated in this book. By using God's Word, you can allow Him to work through you to help your church embrace the concept of vision.

One idea would be to use these studies in a one- or two-day retreat with your leadership team to share God's call to vision.

Other ways to break down barriers to vision in your church:

- Help organize a home Bible study based on the concepts of vision found in this book; use the Bible studies included here as a foundation for the study.
- Encourage the formation of a prayer team that intercedes for you as you search for God's vision in your ministry.

Bible Studies

Each of the following Bible studies has been designed for individual or group use during a 40- to 60-minute session. The questions in each study are intended to help you and your group find out for yourselves what the scriptural passage says in its own context, how it relates to key principles of vision and visionary leadership and how you can apply what you have learned to your church's ministries.

STUDY 1

Vision and Visionary Leadership in the Old Testament

READ PROVERBS 29:18.

The *King James Version* translates Proverbs 29:18, "Where there is no vision, the people perish." The *New International Version* renders the verse, "Where there is no revelation, the people cast off restraint." The Hebrew word *khazon* in Proverbs 29:18 is variously translated "vision" *(KJV, NASB)*, "prophecy" *(RSV)* and "revelation" *(NIV)*. Each of these translations underscores the fact that true vision comes only from the Lord.

1. Compare the various translations of Proverbs 29:18 (*KJV, NIV, NASB,* etc.) and rewrite the verse in your own words.

2. What does this verse say about why you and your church need God's vision for your ministry?

From the following passages of the Old Testament, what can be learned from these people about how the vision God gave them affected their lives?

3. Abraham in Genesis 12:1-3; 15:1-7; 17:1-15. Why did God state and restate three times the vision He gave Abraham? What circumstances and plans in Abraham's life were affected and changed by God's vision for him on each occasion?

4. Moses in Exodus 3:1-10. How much strategic detail did God add to the vision He gave Moses (see Exod. 3:11-22; 4:1-17)?

5. Joshua in Joshua 1:1-5. How much detail is included in God's vision for Joshua about the direction and goals of God's plan to lead Israel into the Promised Land? How is the additional direction from the Lord in Joshua 1:6-9 related to the vision in 1:1-5? How important to the vision was identifying and marshalling resources (see Josh. 1:10-15), gathering information (see Josh. 2:1,22-24) and planning strategically (see Josh. 3:1-4; 6:1-7)?

6. Nehemiah in Nehemiah 2:12. How did Nehemiah receive a vision from the Lord to rebuild the city of Jerusalem (see Neh. 1:3-4; 2:4-5)?

7. David in 1 Samuel 17:34-37,45-48. What attitudes and qualities did David's vision of God's plan for Israel inspire in him (see 1 Sam. 23:15-18)? What attitudes should the vision for ministry God gives you and your church inspire in you?

8. How did God's vision for each of the following prophets cause the prophet to change the way he lived and ministered?

   Isaiah (see Isa. 1:1; 6:1-10)

   Jeremiah (see Jer. 1:4-19)

   Ezekiel (see Ezek. 1:1-28; 2:1-10; 3:4-9)

STUDY 2

Vision and Visionary Leadership in the New Testament

From the following passages of the New Testament, what can be learned from these people about how the vision God gave them affected their lives?

1. Jesus' vision for ministry to the Early Church in Acts 1:4-8. What specific vision had God given His people that began to be fulfilled and implemented on Pentecost in Acts 2:14-22? How was this event related to the vision Jesus gave the Church in Acts 1:4-8?

2. Paul's vision for ministry in Acts 9:15; 26:15-23. How did the vision God gave Paul affect the way he lived and ministered (see 2 Cor. 11:23-28)?

3. Peter's vision for ministry in Acts 10:9-16; 11:4-18. How did God's vision for Peter to evangelize Gentiles restate and underscore Jesus' vision for the ministry and outreach of the Early Church in Acts 1:8? How did it change Peter's plans for evangelism?

4. How was Paul's ministry affected by continuing to receive strategic direction from God in Acts 16:9-10 and 18:9? What does this suggest about continuing to consult God as you implement the vision for ministry He has given you and your church (see Prov. 3:6)?

5. What conclusions can be drawn from these New Testament passages about the way God uses vision?

6. Does God give men who are visionary leaders or prophets to the Church today? Read Ephesians 4:11. Has God left us without vision today?

7. What vision for ministry do you feel God may be giving you and your church?

8. What vision for ministry did God give His Church in Matthew 28:18-20; Luke 24:46-49; Acts 1:8? (Compare Matt. 10:1-8 with 28:18-20; see also Mark 16:15-20; Luke 9:1-6; 10:1-16.) How much strategic detail is included in these passages?

STUDY 3

Receiving God's Vision for Your Ministry

How did the Early Church receive its vision for ministry from God? One account recorded in Acts occurred in A.D. 47 in the city of Antioch in Syria.

READ ACTS 13:1-3.

1. What is the Church doing as the passage unfolds? Describe in your own words what worship is (see Luke 24:52-53; Acts 1:14; 2:42-47; Eph. 5:18-20; Col. 3:16); what fasting is (see 2 Chron. 20:3-4; Acts 14:23).

2. Who was present? Note names. What do these names tell us? What kinds of people are found within the Church?

3. What is the significance of the Holy Spirit's saying "Set them apart"? What is the significance of the laying on of hands?

4. What are some of the tasks of the Church according to this passage?

5. What vision does God's Spirit give to the Church of Antioch with regard to the work to which He called Paul and Barnabas (see Acts 13:2; 19:15; 22:21; 26:16-18)?

6. Has God given you and your church a vision through pointing to a certain person or certain persons whom He has gifted and to whom He has given a burden for a particular ministry?

7. Once the Holy Spirit's direction was stated in Acts 13:2, what did the Church do in 13:3?

8. Were the actions in Acts 13:3 seeking confirmation of the message, or do they reflect hesitation on the part of the Church?

9. What do you feel is the most significant point today's Church should learn from this historical event in Acts 13:1-3?

10. What do James 4:13-15 and Proverbs 3:6 show about implementing and maintaining the vision for ministry God has given you and your church? How does ongoing prayer fit into this process (see Eph. 5:18; Phil. 4:4-7)?

APPENDIX 2

MISSION AND VISION AT BARNA RESEARCH

It is important that we practice what we preach. To give you a sense of how we have made mission and vision work for the Barna Research Group during its 20 years of business and ministry, here are the mission and vision statements that have driven us.

MISSION

To provide excellent marketing research services and counsel—i.e., research design, sampling, data collection, data tabulation, data analysis and interpretation—that helps our clients and produces a reasonable profit.

VISION

To provide current, accurate and reliable information, in bite-sized pieces, and at reasonable costs, to ministry leaders in order to facilitate strategic decision making.

Throughout our history, it is the vision statement that has directed us to do things differently from the other 3,000 marketing research firms in America. We are information merchants, but the information we provide must have the highest level of integrity: We serve a holy and righteous God whose character defines integrity. We strive to help our clients learn as much as they can handle—no more and no less—in order to be good stewards of our skills and efforts, their time and money, and the information generated through the research. We charge what we perceive to be a reasonable rate for our services—not going for all we could get, but giving each client what we truly believe is good value. Our target is ministry leaders—individuals whose primary function is to serve God and His Church, and who have the potential to motivate, mobilize, resource and direct people to pursue God's vision as delivered to the ministry. The desired outcome of the information we deliver is that better decisions will be made than would have otherwise been possible. Those decisions should maximize the strategic possibilities.

We use this vision declaration as a filter through which we make both tactical and strategic decisions. It serves as a yardstick for evaluating our success—that is, our level of obedience to the unique ministry God has provided to us. It has enabled us to reject potentially lucrative projects and various ministry opportunities because they simply were not right for us. And this vision continually motivates us to remain focused on serving God's people for Kingdom purposes.

• •

Appendix 3

Vision and Church Marketing

Let's cut to the heart of the matter. Every church in America is involved in marketing. If you have a lawn sign, advertise in the newspaper or Yellow Pages, have a Friend's Day campaign, provide brochures or other information about your church to visitors, mail a newsletter to members or engage in any of hundreds of other activities designed to attract people to the church, you are marketing your church.

In these few pages, the "should you or shouldn't you" questions related to church marketing will not be addressed. That debate has been adequately addressed in other literature. The focus of this section is upon how well you market your church. The underlying assumption is that, like everything else you undertake, your marketing should be done with the utmost excellence, as if you are engaging in that activity for God, not for men (see Col. 3:23).

Realize that when we are speaking about marketing, it is defined as all of the activities preceding and including a transaction in which two parties willingly exchange resources of commensurate value. When we consider marketing within a church context, we are seeking to persuade people to engage in significant relationships: first and foremost with Jesus Christ, secondarily with other believers.

The Seven Steps

The marketing process entails seven steps. Each step, of course, involves a number of activities. Taken in order and effectively carried out, these steps will lead to effective marketing. The steps are shown in the accompanying chart. Briefly reviewed, marketing requires you to do the following:

1. Collect and Analyze Information

Know the environment in which you have been called to market your product or service. Understand the demographics, values, attitudes and beliefs of the population. Understand the dynamics of your church and its marketing efforts as well as that of your competition. (Remember, your competition is not other churches.) Examine trends and projections about the future concerning needs related to your product area.

2. Articulate Your Vision

Armed with the necessary information—such as market data, God's guidance, the counsel of others, past experience—describe the vision in ways that clarify your purpose, direction and objectives. The vision will act as the filter for all related decision making.

3. Identify Your Resource Base

Given the direction you wish to pursue, you must determine what resources—people, facilities, money, ideas, image and goodwill—you can count on. Those resources will be important in the planning process. While you do not want to limit your ministry by focusing upon resources in hand, neither do you want to waste time and effort devising plans that cannot be carried out because you lack resources.

4. Create Your Marketing Plan

The best marketing is planned. Like the vision, the plan should be written. It must be articulated for, and owned by, all of the pertinent individuals. Included in marketing plans are the goals and objectives of the organization, the strategies to satisfy those desired ends and the tactics to be employed to accommodate those strategies. Budgets and activity schedules are a part of this planning.

5. Communicate and Implement the Plan

The best plans in the world are of no value unless they are put into practice. This requires letting people know the contents of the plan and how they can become part of the process and persuading them to carry out the plan.

6. Seek Feedback as the Plan Is Implemented

During the process, sensitivity to the market is necessary. Plans are attempts to create order out of chaos to achieve desired results. Inevitably, the unforeseen emerges: special circumstances were not anticipated, information was improperly evaluated. Paying attention to the reactions of the target audience allows you to fine-tune your marketing to accommodate new perspectives, unexpected obstacles and unforeseen opportunities.

7. Revise and Reimplement the Plan

When the feedback has been analyzed and its implications determined, the marketing effort should be changed to reflect the new insights. At such transitions, feedback needs to be gained to measure the impact of the change, resulting in further fine-tuning. The cycle goes on this way until either a new vision is created or the plan itself is altered.

The Marketing Process

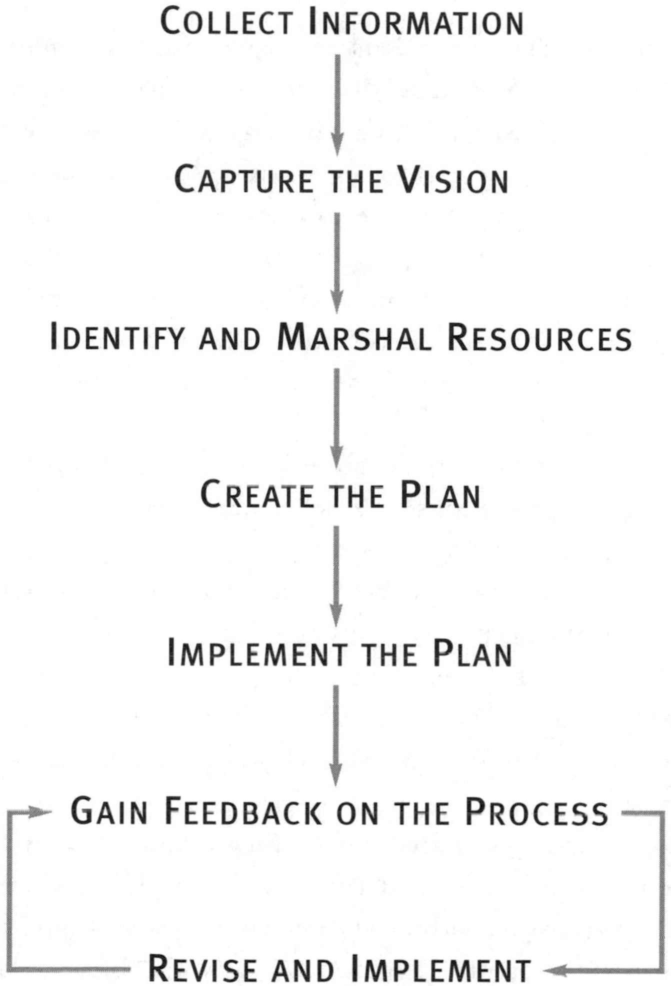

Collect Information

Capture the Vision

Identify and Marshal Resources

Create the Plan

Implement the Plan

Gain Feedback on the Process

Revise and Implement

Marketing Without Vision

Many companies market their products without moving through the seven-step process. In fact, tens of thousands of companies every year attempt to market their products and services without having a vision in place. You can read about these companies. They generally are listed in the rolls of bankrupt organizations. Marketing without cultivating and clarifying your vision is a near-certain prescription for failure.

Here are a few reasons why vision is so critical to successful marketing.

1. **Vision provides the means of organizing information into a meaningful perspective.** One of my favorite verses in the Bible is Ecclesiastes 12:12, which reads, in part, "There is no end of opinions ready to be expressed. Studying them can go on forever, and become very exhausting" *(TLB)*. Without vision, we can fall victim to analysis paralysis or, worse, to data collection insurrection. Vision makes the information you gather purposeful. It provides a reason for generating the information and a framework for analyzing and applying it.
2. **Vision integrates your mission with existing opportunities.** Many organizations have viable mission statements. But when it comes time to act out those missions, they are left flapping in the breeze. Why? Because they do not have the specificity provided by a vision statement. Without the vision, they are powerless to become anything more than all things to all people; such efforts generally result in being nothing to everybody. Vision provides the necessary direction and detail to mission.
3. **Vision is the key ingredient to formulating a plan for action.** Your marketing plan consists of strategies and tactics. Unless you have a clearly articulated vision, you have no basis upon which to create strategies. Your goals and objectives lack any realistic context. Marketing becomes a free-for-all in which the loudest voice or the deepest pocket gets its way. Vision is

the unifying factor that directs the course of the planning discussion and acts as the filter for all ideas.

4. **Without vision, the communication of the marketing plan sounds like good works performed for their own sake.** The driving force must be vision; otherwise, marketing efforts can appear to be (or truly will become) simple exercises in marketing technique. And there is little that proves to be as self-defeating as marketing that lacks heart. The vision is that heart. Especially in a church context, vision is the catalyst to effective outreach—i.e., ministry that takes place to glorify God rather than to serve people's personal or corporate desires.
5. **Vision acts as a filter for evaluating feedback.** Often, church leaders receive reactions from the congregation and outsiders about the marketing and ministry activities of the church. If those reactions are negative, the leaders may respond by changing the activities of the church to avoid repeated negative feedback. There may be times when people criticize the church's ministry or marketing activities, even though those activities are concurrent with the church's vision. The vision acts as a filter for evaluating such criticism. Instead of changing the ministry activities in response to negative feedback, the leaders can maintain their focus on the vision and move ahead in consistent and effective ministry.

Think of it this way: Marketing without vision is like sending a construction team into the Sahara Desert with vague instructions to build a luxury hotel but without blueprints for the project. First, it is an activity that lacks a significant purpose (would you stay in a hotel in the middle of the Sahara?). Second, it cannot be satisfactorily accomplished because there is neither a realistic plan nor a viable understanding of how, why and for whom the project will be completed. Third, this project represents bad stewardship. God's vision for ministry never calls for resources to be wasted.

APPENDIX 4

WHAT IF?

Let me tackle five common objections that pastors and church leaders have raised regarding the necessity of having God's vision for ministry.

TIMING

Q: What if it is the appropriate time of the year to develop and begin implementing the church's ministry plan (i.e., marketing plan), but we do not have a clear vision?

A: Put the church in a holding pattern in terms of marketing and expend all your energies on clarifying God's vision for the ministry. Do whatever is reasonable to make things flow smoothly in the short term. Do not make any long-term obligations until your vision is intact.

How can you focus energy on grasping the vision when that is the responsibility of the senior pastor? The congregation ought to pray diligently for the pastor as he or she pursues the vision. Individuals can help gather the necessary background information for context for vision (e.g., community demographics, congregational statistics). Those people who can provide wise, godly counsel should be contacted and made available as the pastor needs them. The church can release the pastor, temporarily, from those duties that can be fulfilled by others, encouraging him or her to concentrate on grasping God's vision.

Demonstrate maximum intelligence by not waiting for the planning crunch to roll around. Start now to evaluate whether your planning sessions will be guided by an authentic vision for ministry. If not, start the vision-capturing process immediately.

Agreement

Q: What if the vision espoused by the pastor contradicts the church's current marketing activities?

A: Always err on the side of your vision. If there is any doubt, opt for the alternative that best reflects the vision. Marketing, by the seven-step process defined in appendix 3, must fit within the scope of the vision rather than redefine it. If the marketing activities of the church do not coincide with the vision, the head marketer or decision maker in the church must terminate those activities being conducted on behalf of the church but that are outside the boundaries of the vision.

Resources

Q: What if God truly imparted a big vision to us, and we just don't have the money to pull it off this year?

A: Vision is a long-term process. It is implemented incrementally. You should be concerned if your leaders come back with a plan that indicates the vision can be fulfilled within a year or two. That suggests that either the vision was too small, the planners do not understand the vision, or the planners are unrealistic or do not have a clue about the planning process.

Think of your activities this year as being partially geared to satisfying the vision and partially geared to laying a foundation for future years of ministry.

Interpretation

Q: What if different people involved in the marketing process arrive at different interpretations of the vision?

A: Technically, this is impossible. If God has imparted the vision to the senior pastor, then that pastor must interpret the vision for the rest of the church. It is not up to individual marketers to arrive at independent interpretations. It is their responsibility to develop objectives, strategies and tactics based on the *official* interpretation of the vision, which will enable the vision to become reality.

VEHICLE

Q: What if the senior pastor is vision-driven but disdains marketing, planning and other "worldly" contrivances?

A: Challenge the pastor to explain how orderly, timely progress can be made without a tangible plan built upon the vision. Ask for examples of churches where his approach has worked smoothly. Ask for any type of scholarly papers or case studies that support that approach. Ask for biblical reasoning. Do not accept the usual, paper-thin, superspiritual retorts that are aggressively offensive (e.g., "If you had the faith of a mustard seed, you would let Him take care of the marketing.").

The New Testament is filled with examples of God's people authentically following Him and being involved in the solution to their problems. Luke 14:28-30 records the parable of counting the cost, which encourages people to plan. If the pastor cannot support the development of a plan, he cannot create a team of ministers. That leads to an attenuated church, a one-man show in which confusion and anarchy reign. If the pastor is incapable of leading, he might be better off at a church that is more comfortable with a hands-off style of management.

In the end, realize that vision is the core of marketing. All marketing efforts must be consistent with the vision.

. . . .

APPENDIX 5

OTHER RESOURCES

Each of the books listed below provides some useful insights into vision. While most of them were not written from a Christian perspective nor designed to address the unique needs of a ministry, the techniques and ideas related to vision raised in these books may provide some further insight.

From a Christian Perspective

Barna, George. *Turning Vision into Action.* Ventura, CA: Regal Books, 1996.

Chand, Samuel, and Cecil Murphey. *Futuring.* Grand Rapids, MI: Baker Books, 2002.

Malphurs, Aubrey. *Developing Vision for Ministry.* Grand Rapids, MI: Baker Books, 1992.

Stanley, Andy. *Visioneering.* Sisters, OR: Multnomah Publishers, 1999.

Sweet, Leonard. *Carpe Mañana.* Grand Rapids, MI: Zondervan Publishing House, 2001.

From a Business Perspective

Abrahams, Jeffrey. *The Mission Statement Book.* Berkeley, CA: Ten Speed Press, 1995.

Barker, Joel. *Future Edge.* New York: William Morrow and Company, 1992.

———. *Paradigms.* New York: Harper Business, 1993.

Gibson, Rowan, ed. *Rethinking the Future.* London: Nicholas Brealey Publishing, 1999.

Hamel, Gary. *Leading the Revolution.* Boston: Harvard Business School Press, 2000.

Kawasaki, Guy. *Selling the Dream.* New York: Harper Collins, 1991.

Kelley, Tom. *The Art of Innovation.* New York: Doubleday Currency Books, 2001.

Nanus, Burt. *Visionary Leadership.* San Francisco: Jossey-Bass, 1992.

Schwartz, Peter. *The Art of the Long View.* New York: Doubleday Currency Books, 1991.

Wacker, Watts, and Jim Taylor. *The Visionary's Handbook.* New York: Harper Business, 2000.

About the Barna Research Group

The Barna Research Group is a marketing research firm located in Ventura, California. It is dedicated to serving clients by providing current, accurate and reliable information, in bite-sized pieces, at reasonable cost, to facilitate strategic decision making.

Established in 1984 by George and Nancy Barna, the company has been honored to serve thousands of clients through primary research, consulting and seminars, working with for-profit and nonprofit organizations. Among the for-profit clients served are American Express, Federal Express, Ford Motor Company, Hyatt Hotels, Pearle Vision Centers, Prudential, Ramada Inns, Southwestern Bell Telephone, Visa U.S.A. and The Walt Disney Company. Among the nonreligious, nonprofit organizations served have been Boys and Girls Clubs, CARE, Easter Seals, Feed the Children, KidsPeace and the U.S. Army. Barna Research has served several thousand churches and more than 300 parachurch ministries such as American Bible Society, Billy Graham Association, Campus Crusade for Christ, Compassion International, Focus on the Family, InterVarsity, Josh McDowell Ministries, Prison Fellowship, Salvation Army, World Vision and Youth for Christ.

The organization is well known for helping Christian ministries stay alert to changes and opportunities in American society. The group develops resources for Christian ministries and provides a wealth of free, current information online (www.barna.org), including the publication of its latest findings in a free biweekly report (*The Barna Update*). More than 1 million copies of resources produced by Barna Research have been purchased to help organizations be more effective in their work.

Resources

Newsletter

The Barna Update, produced every two weeks, is available for free online at www.barna.org. To sign up for a free subscription to these topical research reports, go to the website.

Books (by George Barna)

Think Like Jesus (Integrity Publishers, 2003)
Transforming Children into Spiritual Champions (Issachar Resources, 2003)
Single Focus (Regal Books, 2003)
Growing Your Church from the Outside In (Regal Books, 2002)
A Fish out of Water (Integrity Publishers, 2002)
The Power of Team Leadership (WaterBrook Press, 2001)
Growing True Disciples (WaterBrook Press, 2001)
Boiling Point (Regal Books, 2001)
Real Teens (Regal Books, 2001)
The Habits of Highly Effective Churches (Regal Books, 2000)

Also available are videocassette and audiocassette presentations by George Barna.

To learn more about Barna Research, please visit www.barna.org or call 1-800-55-BARNA.